Chapter 1: The Encrypted Message

Alex Carter sat alone in his dimly lit study, surrounded by stacks of books on cryptography and computer science. He had always preferred the company of numbers and codes over people. It was safer that way. On this particular day, however, a simple ping from his computer signaled something unusual. When he turned to his screen, he found an unread message waiting for him—a message that would change everything.

The message was unlike anything he had encountered before. It was highly encrypted, filled with layers of codes, symbols, and puzzles that seemed both intricate and purposeful. The sender remained anonymous, which only heightened the mystery. Instinctively, Alex knew he should ignore it, dismiss it as a prank, but he felt a strong pull towards it, like a magnet drawing him in. The thrill of solving a puzzle was often overpowering.

As he leaned closer to the screen, Alex felt his heartbeat quicken. He had always been intrigued by the art of cryptography, a field that intertwines mathematics, linguistics, and art. It requires both logical reasoning and a creative mind. This was not just a message; it was a challenge. Maybe that was why he couldn't look away. He pushed aside his qualms and decided to immerse himself in it.

Alex knew he had the skills to decrypt the message. He opened his toolset, a collection of software and algorithms he had built over the years. With the right conditions, he could break down the encryption structure. First, he needed to identify the type of encryption used. There are many methods—symmetric, asymmetric, or even some contemporary algorithms like AES. This was a problem that demanded his expertise and intense focus.

Once he had narrowed the possibilities, Alex began to methodically break the code down. He spent hours analyzing the patterns and structures of the symbols, looking for clues. He used frequency analysis to examine the letter combinations, something cryptographers often employ. In this way, he started to get a clearer picture of what the message might be communicating.

With each passing moment, his initial apprehension melted away. Instead, he felt a sense of excitement that he hadn't felt in years. The cryptographic puzzles were like a dance, each step revealing another layer to the intricate choreography of information. He immersed himself in the complex world of digits and letters, driven by the thrill of discovery.

As he delved deeper, the message slowly began to unravel. It revealed fragments of words, and soon he noticed a particular configuration that pointed towards a historical event. This discovery intrigued him even further. Was this just an elaborate game or was there a serious purpose behind it? He began to take notes, meticulously documenting his findings, ensuring he would not lose track of any detail.

After hours of hard work, Alex finally broke a significant part of the code. There seemed to be references to a location, coordinates that suggested a place he knew well. It was a dilapidated building on the outskirts of town, long abandoned and filled with whispers of the past. An unsettling feeling enveloped him. Why would someone send him a message like this? What were they trying to achieve?

His mind raced with questions, each one more perplexing than the last. With every layer he peeled back, he unearthed new mysteries and hidden meanings. The thrill of the chase was intoxicating. But along with that thrill came a tinge of fear. Who was sending this message? What was their intention? Was he about to tiptoe into a situation far greater than he ever anticipated?

Alex couldn't help but consider the risks involved. He thought about the implications of following this thread. It could lead him to something dangerous. He remembered stories he had read of other cryptographers getting too close to secrets they should have left alone. But then again, the very thing that excited him was the unknown. Did he have the strength to turn away now that he was so deeply entrenched in this puzzle?

He leaned back in his chair, mixing thoughts of intrigue and dread. There was also the opportunity to learn more about advanced cryptographic techniques and methods that he could perhaps use for his own projects. The lure of knowledge is strong for a reclusive mind like his. He revisited the thought of the abandoned building, mulling over the potential discoveries waiting for him there.

After a short break, Alex made a decision. He would go to the location noted in the message. He would approach it cautiously, but he felt he couldn't leave this mystery unattended. There was a potential treasure trove of information just waiting for him. Yet, he felt it was equally important to remain vigilant and aware of his surroundings.

With new resolve, Alex prepared to leave his study. He gathered a few essentials—his laptop, a notebook, and a pen. He also grabbed a flashlight, just in case the building was as dark and decrepit as he imagined. Each item felt like a tool in his arsenal, bringing him closer to the truth.

As he drove towards the coordinates, the streets gradually transformed from the familiarity of the city to the eerie quiet of the outskirts. Every minute felt like an hour, layered with anticipation, anxiety, and a thirst for answers. He wondered if he would find clues, or if he was merely following the whims of a mischievous ghost.

Upon arriving at the location, Alex stepped out of the car, taking a deep breath. The building loomed in front of him, a mere shadow of its former self. The windows were shattered, and vines crept along its weathered walls. It felt both foreboding and strangely inviting, as if it held secrets yet to be revealed.

He approached the entrance cautiously, unsure of what he would find inside. With his flashlight switched on, he took a step into the darkness. The air was heavy with dust and the scent of decay. The beams of light from his flashlight danced across the walls, illuminating forgotten memories stored within.

As he moved about, he noted the remnants of documents scattered across the floor. They bore names and dates that hinted at a forgotten past intertwined with the present mystery. He could feel every hair on his body standing on end, as though the very walls were alive with stories waiting to be uncovered.

The message that had drawn him here was clearly more than just a game. Alex's mind whirred with questions, theories, and plans as he searched through the debris, piecing together the fragmented past that lay before him. The thrill of the unknown propelled him onward, and he felt, for the first time in many years, that he was exactly where he needed to be.

Chapter 2: The Codebreaker's Dilemma

Alex sat at his desk, staring at the screen before him. He had encountered many codes in his time, but none like this. The lines of text seemed to swirl and shift, each symbol taunting him with its mystery. As he began to analyze the first segment, he felt an unsettling mix of excitement and dread. Each new finding only deepened the complexity, and soon he found himself caught in a web of symbols that seemed to have no end.

Sleepless nights became common for Alex. He would pour over the code for hours, his eyes straining against the glow of the monitor. Coffee cups piled around him, remnants of his attempts to stay alert. The quiet of the night was only broken by the occasional click of the keyboard as he typed out his thoughts and findings. He was on the edge of understanding but always felt a step behind. It was as if the code itself was a living entity, constantly shifting to evade his grasp.

As he delved deeper into his work, he began to sense that there was much more at stake than just solving a puzzle. The weight of the code pressed on him like a heavy blanket, suffocating yet compelling. His research turned into an obsession. He started to connect the dots, realizing that the symbols could be pointing to something significant. He felt like a detective, piecing together clues that could lead to a larger story. As he worked, he jotted down notes, sketching connections between different segments of the code, trying to make sense of the chaos.

One night, as the clock ticked past midnight, Alex hit a breakthrough. He had been staring at a series of letters that made little sense when suddenly, a pattern emerged. It was subtle, almost hidden in plain sight. He grabbed a piece of paper and scribbled down the sequence, realizing it resembled a numeric pattern he had seen in an earlier project. Excitement surged through him; this could be crucial to understanding the code's purpose. With each new reveal, he felt more and more assured that he was close to uncovering something monumental.

However, the more he learned, the more he realized that he was not alone in this endeavor. Whispers of others working on similar codes reached him through online forums and message boards. Some shared their frustrations; others discussed their findings. Alex found himself drawn to these discussions, feeling a sense of camaraderie with fellow codebreakers. They exchanged theories and approached the work with various levels of expertise. Each conversation added another layer to his understanding, reinforcing the idea that this was a collective effort.

Yet, even within this community, Alex sensed an undercurrent of competition. Some participants seemed more interested in fame than the purpose of their work. Codebreaking had always been a solitary pursuit for Alex, and now the social dynamics added a new layer of complexity. He often debated whether he should share his findings or keep them close to his chest. With each passing day, he felt the pressure build. The stakes were high, and the implications of what he found could have serious consequences.

As weeks turned into months, Alex continued working tirelessly on the code. He learned to compartmentalize his thoughts, focusing on one section at a time. He drafted various hypotheses, mentioning in his notes possible links to national security, technology, and cryptography. The idea of being part of something bigger, something that could affect many lives, weighed heavily on him. Each time he uncovered a new layer, he sensed that he was close to something that could change the course of history.

Alex decided to take a step back and reevaluate his approach. He mapped out his findings visually, creating a wall of interconnected notes and diagrams. This helped him see the relationships between different segments clearly. He sought advice from experts online, asking for feedback on his methods and conclusions. Their insights provided him with fresh perspectives, sparking new ideas that he had not considered before.

One afternoon, while sorting through the maze of papers covering his desk, Alex discovered an unusual entry. He noted a series of dates correlated with key historical events. It was intriguing how these dates lined up perfectly with some of the code's most complicated segments. As he delved deeper, he began to connect the dots, identifying similar patterns that could hold historical significance. This was not just a code; it was a narrative, telling a story hidden beneath layers of encryption.

As he pieced together the historical references, his mind raced with possibilities. Could this be a warning? A message meant for someone? He decided to reach out to a historian he had spoken with previously, hoping to glean more information about the events and their contexts. They engaged in a thoughtful discussion, exploring different angles and interpretations of the dates. The historian's enthusiasm fueled Alex's desire to dig even deeper.

The more Alex explored, the more he realized the potential implications of his findings. A knot of anxiety tightened in his stomach as he considered the ramifications of what he might be on the verge of uncovering. Would his work lead to a monumental discovery or a tangled mess of false leads? Despite the uncertainty, he was determined to follow the trail wherever it might lead.

Days turned into weeks, and the overtime paid off. Alex gathered enough data to compile a report summarizing his findings. It wasn't just about the code anymore; it was about the connections, the potential histories wrapped within those lines. He dedicated countless hours to clarifying his thoughts, ensuring every point was articulated clearly to illustrate the importance of what he had discovered.

Throughout this process, Alex also kept track of his emotional journey. It was not easy, wrestling with the demands of his work while keeping a steady mind. He set regular breaks to recharge, found comfort in taking walks outside, and sought moments of stillness to help him process everything. This new balance proved essential, allowing him to return to his work with a fresh perspective and renewed energy.

It was during one of these breaks, on a crisp autumn afternoon, that Alex fully grasped the depth of what he was working with. The leaves crunched beneath his feet as he walked, giving way to a moment of clarity. There was an urgency to his task, and it was spurred by a drive to make sense of chaos. Solving the code was becoming a part of him, a mission he could not abandon. He had to uncover the truth, no matter the cost.

The journey was still ongoing. New questions emerged daily, and the code remained elusive. However, Alex felt a sense of purpose that fueled his determination. The sleepless nights seemed less daunting, and he found motivation in each minor discovery, recognizing that every small step brought him closer to understanding a much bigger picture. Each line of code, each symbol, and every sleepless night was leading him deeper into the heart of the mystery.

Chapter 3: A Hidden Warning

Alex sat in front of his computer, fingers hovering over the keyboard. The room was dimly lit, and the glow from the screen illuminated his focused expression. He had been working tirelessly to decode a set of complex algorithms that had baffled many before him. The promise of discovery danced in his mind, but so did an uneasy feeling in the pit of his stomach. He read about others who had tried to decipher the same code, only to have vanished without a trace.

Just as he was about to dive deeper into the strings of numbers and letters, a message popped up on his screen. It was an anonymous chat message from a hacker going by the name Cipher. The words were simple, yet they sent a chill down Alex's spine: "People who have tried to crack this code have disappeared." Those words lingered in the air, heavy with implication. Who was this Cipher? A friend or a foe?

Curiosity mixed with caution. Alex took a moment to consider the implications of Cipher's message. He had heard stories of hackers like Cipher—people who blended skill with a streak of danger. It was a world full of shadows and secrets. He had hesitated to reach out for help, believing it was a sign of weakness. Yet here was Cipher, offering assistance when Alex needed it most. The dilemma was real.

Alex decided to respond, asking Cipher how he knew about those who had disappeared. The typing indicator blinked for a second, and then a response came through, simple yet packed with gravity. Cipher explained that he had been tracking the code for several months. He told Alex about the strange occurrences surrounding the individuals who had tried to crack the code. His words painted a picture of foreboding—each night, they would become increasingly obsessed, losing sleep, friends, and eventually their lives. It was as if the code held a hidden curse.

Despite the warnings, Alex felt an undeniable urge to learn more, to uncover the truth behind the code. The desire to decode the message was like a fire within him, and the thought of backing down was impossible. But there was another part of him that screamed to walk away. If Cipher was right, this could lead to a path of danger that no one wanted to follow. Alex weighed his options carefully.

He hesitated for a moment, lost in thought. What if it was all a hoax? What if Cipher was simply trying to scare him, to manipulate him into abandoning his quest? At the same time, what if this hacker was telling the truth? There was an inherent risk in the unknown. Maybe it would be best to research Cipher's background.

To dig deeper, Alex carefully searched online, looking for mentions of Cipher. He combed through various forums, checking for any information on the mysterious hacker. He noted that many people had expressed admiration for Cipher's skills, but there were also whispers of dubious acts and questionable ethics. The lines were blurred, and as he searched for truth, he could feel the weight of uncertainty pressing down on him.

After several hours, Alex returned to his computer. He weighed his options. Could he really trust Cipher? The thought was scary, yet he also pondered: what if he didn't take that chance? After all, this could mean the difference between solving the code and disappearing just like those before him. He made a decision and typed out another message to Cipher, asking for more details about the disappearances.

The response was almost immediate. Cipher shared a list of names and the stories behind each of them. Alex's heart raced. These were individuals who were real, with backgrounds and lives just like his. Cipher recounted tales of how they had become consumed by their work, gradually isolating themselves from family and friends. The drive to finish consumed them. He even told stories of those who had been found wandering in a daze, utterly lost and unable to recall their past.

There was a sinister tone to Cipher's revelations. Each person's tale was distinct but shared common threads of obsession and despair.

It was chilling to think that one could go from being a successful coder to being a ghost lost to the world.

Still, there was a part of Alex that refused to believe in fear. Perhaps Cipher just wanted to control a narrative that played to his advantage. However, he couldn't shake the feeling of urgency that accompanied each of Cipher's tales.

The stakes were becoming higher. As Alex contemplated his next steps, he considered the possibility of collaborating with Cipher. There was safety in numbers—the thought of tackling the code with someone who had insider knowledge around it struck a chord. He was cautious, but what did he have to lose?

After pondering for a while, Alex found himself typing again. He proposed the idea to Cipher. He suggested a partnership, believing that together they could face the puzzle without succumbing to the madness that affected those before them. He pressed send before his mind could convince him otherwise.

Cipher replied quickly, agreeing with an air of confidence. The hacker explained that he, too, had been intrigued by the challenge and had spent countless hours scrutinizing the same code. Together, they could unravel its mysteries or at least share the burden of the pursuit. The proposition made Alex feel a pang of excitement amid the fear.

Over the next few days, the two conversed regularly. Cipher detailed methods he used for decryption. They exchanged ideas and theories while Alex constantly weighed the possibility that the hacker could not be trusted. Each discussion brought with it a blend of anticipation and anxiety. Cipher urged Alex to push deeper into the code but also warned him about watching over his shoulder.

Despite the risks, the thrill of collaboration emboldened Alex. The knowledge that someone else was in the same boat made the code less daunting. They spent hours running simulations and breaking down the algorithms. Ideas flowed from one to the other, like electricity sparking in the air. They lost track of time and of the world outside.

However, as they worked, the warnings from Cipher echoed louder. Days turned into sleepless nights, and Alex began to feel the effects of his obsession. He noticed he was becoming less connected to reality. Friends reached out with questions, but he merely brushed them off, doubling down on his work. It was exhilarating and terrifying all at once.

Soon, he found that the lines between reality and obsession began to blur. Moments of clarity were fleeting, and he was filled with dread when he noticed strange occurrences—objects misplaced, shadows lurking in the corner of his vision. He shook his head, chastising himself for giving in to paranoia. Still, a small part of him couldn't help but wonder if he was falling into the same trap that had ensnared those before him.

As he progressed, he would share his findings with Cipher. Sometimes their exchanges would be filled with excitement, but other times, Cipher would offer words dripping with caution. It became a dark game of cat and mouse—a journey filled with discovery but marred by whispers of lurking dangers.

The partnership was intense and, at times, overwhelming. What started as friendly exchanges over algorithms morphed into urgent discussions about their futures and mental states. Cipher insisted they take breaks, encouraging Alex to step away and clear his mind, but Alex resisted. The dance of obsession was intoxicating, and he feared that taking a break could lead to losing momentum.

Days turned into a haze of code, caffeine, and the constant hum of alerts from the computer. As Alex felt himself spiraling deeper, he began reflecting on his decisions. Had he become like those he so deeply feared? Was he able to trust Cipher, or had he inadvertently opened a door that should have remained closed?

And so, the story continued, threaded with warnings of what lies beyond the pursuit of knowledge. The lines were drawn, the masks worn, and the hidden truths waiting just below the surface. Alex knew he stood at a precipice, peering into an abyss filled with shadows, unsure of what awaited him on the other side. The dance with danger was intense, but he was unable to step back. The only question left was how far he was willing to go.

Chapter 4: The Hacker's Network

Alex felt a surge of excitement as he stepped further into the hacker underground. This place was unlike anything he had ever encountered. The atmosphere buzzed with energy, filled with whispers of coded language and hidden schemes. With Cipher's connections, he had access to resources and information that would have been nearly impossible to obtain otherwise. He knew he had to be careful, though. The hacker community operated under a strict code of secrecy and trust, and one misstep could lead to dire consequences.

He started by visiting a low-lit café that served as a meeting point for hackers. The place was full of people typing on laptops, their fingers flying across the keys as they communicated with the outside world. Alex took a seat in a corner and ordered a black coffee. While he waited, he scanned the room, looking for a familiar face. He kept his hood up, trying to blend in. The last thing he wanted was to draw attention to himself.

As he sipped his coffee, he spotted a figure in a leather jacket. It was Cipher, who had arranged to meet him. Cipher had been a mentor to Alex, teaching him the ins and outs of the underground world. When Cipher approached, he had an air of confidence about him. He slid into the seat across from Alex and looked around to ensure no one was eavesdropping.

"Have you found anything yet?" Cipher asked, his voice low and serious.

Alex leaned in closer, eager to share what he had uncovered. He explained that during his last research session, he stumbled upon a message that hinted at a shadowy organization behind the scenes of several leading tech companies. This organization seemed to be influencing major decisions and pushing agendas that were not in the public eye. Alex knew that getting to the bottom of this could expose significant corruption, but it also posed serious risks.

Cipher nodded, intrigued. "Do you think they're involved in hacking, or are they something worse?"

Alex thought for a moment before answering. "It's hard to say. The message implied they had deep connections, almost like they were puppeteering the companies from behind a curtain. They might be gathering intelligence through hackers or using technology to manipulate systems."

Cipher considered this as he finished his coffee. "We need to dig deeper. I have a few contacts who might have more info on this group. They operate in different circles, but they may offer some insights."

After their meeting, Alex felt both anxious and exhilarated. They were stepping into a world much darker and more complex than he had anticipated. He began to reach out to Cipher's contacts, using encrypted messaging to maintain his privacy. Each conversation opened doors to new leads. He learned about people working on the fringes, exposing corruption, and resisting major corporations that took advantage of regular folks.

One contact was a woman named Ada, who had extensive knowledge of corporate hacking. She operated a small forum where she shared intel on tech companies' wrongdoings. Ada had a reputation for being fiercely protective of her sources, and for good reason. Many who crossed her would disappear, either into the shadows or the legal system. Alex felt a combination of respect and fear when he reached out to her.

When he finally got a reply from Ada, she agreed to meet him. They chose a public library as a neutral ground. Alex arrived early, fidgeting with his phone, hoping to keep his nerves in check. When Ada walked in, he noticed she had an air of authority about her. She was deliberate in her movements, and her sharp eyes took in every detail around her.

They found a quiet corner where no one would overhear their conversation. Ada wasted no time. "I hear you're looking into the shadows. Be careful where you tread, kid. There are players in this game who don't like being exposed."

Alex nodded, understanding the weight of her words. He explained his findings and shared his growing suspicion about the organization behind the tech companies. Ada listened intently and then leaned in closer.

"I've seen some things," she said, her voice barely above a whisper. "Tech companies collaborate with this group. They manipulate data, sway public opinion, and control resources. They can sink or swim any idea or product that comes their way. You're not just looking at hackers; you're opening a door to corporate espionage."

Her words sent a chill down Alex's spine. He asked if she had any evidence or connections that could help them track this organization down. Ada hesitated before handing him a set of encrypted files. "This is a risk for both of us, but maybe it will lead you where you need to go. Just remember, the deeper you go, the more difficult it'll be to climb back out."

As Alex reviewed the files, he realized he had stumbled onto something significant. There was coded language in the documents that referred to operations conducted under the radar, away from the public eye. In one section, it described a project that involved manipulating online narratives to influence consumer behavior. This was a clear indication of how far the organization had infiltrated the tech world.

Encouraged by Ada's information, Alex started piecing together the threads. He took meticulous notes, transforming the chaos of data into a comprehensible narrative. He began mapping connections between various tech giants and the unknown organization. Each connection revealed was a step deeper into the labyrinth of the hacker's network.

To gather more information, Alex decided to utilize social engineering. He practiced identifying weaknesses within corporate systems and explored how he might exploit them for information. He created a fake identity online that would allow him to infiltrate forums and chat rooms where insiders communicated. He needed to become a ghost, someone who existed without a trace while still pushing forward in his investigation.

As he continued his search, Alex found a group of rogue hackers who claimed to expose corruption within corporations, operating under a banner of anonymity. They referred to themselves as "The Watchers." Alex contacted them, curious if they had information about the organization tied to the tech companies. They agreed to meet him, but specified they required proof of loyalty before sharing any intel.

Unsure what they expected from him, Alex prepared himself. He already had evidence from Ada's files that showcased potential corrupt practices. He hoped this would be enough to gain their trust. The meeting took place in a secluded location, away from prying eyes. As he entered, he felt a mixture of fear and exhilaration, knowing he was stepping further into the depths of the hacker underworld.

Once inside, Alex was confronted by a small group of masked individuals. They eyed him suspiciously as he presented his case. He laid out the evidence clearly, detailing the ways tech companies were manipulating public opinion and hiding their actions behind the scenes. The more he spoke, the more the tension in the room lifted.

"You're onto something," one of the members finally said. "We have our own intel that supports this. We've seen similar patterns and have been tracking movements for months. Welcome to The Watchers."

This new association presented Alex with both an opportunity and a significant risk. He was now part of a larger mission, one that sought to expose corruption on a grand scale. The further he ventured into this world, the more he realized that uncovering the truth came with perilous stakes. Yet, the desire to bring light to the dark corners of the tech industry fueled his determination.

As Alex delved deeper into the hacker network, he uncovered layers of deception, manipulation, and power struggles that existed behind the scenes. Each revelation only further motivated him to seek out the truth, no matter the cost. He understood that the journey was only beginning, and so many secrets remained hidden beneath the surface.

Chapter 5: The First Threat

Alex lived a typical life in his small, cluttered apartment. He spent most days focused on his work, often finding solace in the many gadgets scattered around his living space. His computer, which was the heart of his projects, was his constant companion. From coding new programs to troubleshooting issues for clients, Alex had built a routine that he cherished. But one fateful afternoon, as he entered his apartment after a long day, he immediately sensed something was off.

The first hint came from the eerie silence that enveloped the space. The usual hum of his computer was absent. Alex stepped inside cautiously, taking in the disarray. Papers were strewn across the floor, and the flickering lights overhead cast unsettling shadows. Each step he took filled him with growing dread. Rushing to his desk, his heart sank. His laptop was smashed, and his other electronics lay in ruins around him. His once tidy workspace had turned into a chaotic scene of destruction.

In the midst of the wreckage, Alex spotted a piece of paper lying on the ground. With trembling hands, he picked it up. The note was cryptic yet unmistakable. "Stop working on the code or there will be consequences." The message sent chills down his spine. Who would break into his home and leave such a threat? The reality of the situation unfolded before him like a nightmare. He wasn't just dealing with random vandalism; this was personal, aimed directly at him.

As he processed the note's contents, Alex realized the urgency of the situation. He had been working on a project that could revolutionize the tech industry, but it had also drawn the attention of powerful people. He had brushed off the occasional unsettling email and strange phone calls, but now he understood that he had crossed a line. The stakes were higher than he had imagined, and he felt a mix of fear and determination. There was no turning back now.

Fearing for his safety, Alex decided he couldn't stay in the apartment any longer. Packing a few essentials, he contemplated where to go. After a moment, he reached out to his friend Jamie, who lived a few blocks away. He could trust Jamie to help him figure things out. Alex quickly texted, asking if he could crash for a few days. Without hesitation, Jamie replied with an enthusiastic "Of course!"

Arriving at Jamie's apartment provided a momentary sense of respite. At least he wasn't alone. After explaining the break-in and the threatening note, Jamie listened intently, concerned wrinkles forming on his forehead. Together, they brainstormed possible explanations for the incident. "Do you have any enemies in your work?" Jamie asked. Alex couldn't pinpoint any specific person, but he knew he had been in heated discussions about the project. It was innovative, and not everyone had been supportive.

Over the next few days, the fear of being followed nagged at Alex. Each time he heard footsteps in the hallway or saw a shadow pass by the window, his heart raced. With Jamie's encouragement, he started to investigate. He combed through his emails and noticed a pattern. A few accounts had been sending vague threats, but he had dismissed them as spam. Now, they seemed to be part of a bigger picture.

The following week, Alex and Jamie chose to deepen their search. They stayed up late, pouring over every detail. They researched the companies that expressed interest—both positive and negative.

They compiled a list of individuals who had shown hostility towards Alex's ideas. It was exhausting work, fueled by coffee and late-night snacks, but they felt a sense of purpose. They were piecing together a puzzle amidst a backdrop of uncertainty and fear.

One evening, they decided to confront the issue more directly. Armed with phone records and email threads, they organized a plan to reach out to those who had made threats. Having Jamie present gave Alex the courage he needed. "Let's send a polite email and see who responds," Jamie suggested. Alex agreed, feeling that taking action might provide a sense of control in a spiraling situation.

They crafted a careful message, outlining Alex's commitment to his work while highlighting the importance of professional integrity. They sent it to a select few who had raised concerns. To their surprise, one individual replied almost immediately. The tone was dismissive, and it only heightened their worries. The sender claimed Alex was not being taken seriously and that he should learn to let go of "pipe dreams."

The return email sparked a heated discussion between Alex and Jamie. "What if this is linked to the break-in?" Alex wondered aloud. Jamie agreed, and they made a list of potential contacts to investigate further. As they continued to dig deeper into the matter, Alex learned that the technology he was working on could disrupt certain markets. This knowledge both terrified and motivated him to keep pushing forward.

Days turned into weeks, and the threat loomed large. Although life continued, the specter of danger lingered over Alex's every move. He began to notice strange cars parked outside his apartment, and twice he felt like someone was watching him from a distance. These experiences were unsettling but only strengthened his resolve. He could not let fear dictate his actions; he had to protect his work and his future.

Alex decided to take further precautions. He consulted with a friend who worked in security. They outlined simple but effective steps. He changed his passwords, added two-factor authentication to his accounts, and even considered a security system for his apartment. Each step they took helped to decrease his anxiety, though the shadow of the potential threat still lingered.

While Alex focused on safety, Jamie remained a loyal ally by his side. They spent time on late-night brainstorming sessions to enhance Alex's project further and enhance its security. Each completed task felt like a victory against the unseen threat. Alex learned to code with increased attention, making sure to keep his files secure.

Amidst the chaos, Alex found solace in the supportive environment he and Jamie fostered. The bond they shared deepened, reinforced by their joint struggle against this looming threat. Every day brought new fears, but it also pushed Alex to channel his energy into his work. The chaotic environment became an unlikely source of inspiration.

However, Alex knew he couldn't hide forever. He had to confront the issue head-on, but when and how remained uncertain. His thoughts swirled, filled with equal parts fear and determination. Soon enough, he would need to make a decision and decide what he was willing to risk for his passion. Life was irrevocably different, and every moment mattered now more than ever. With Jamie by his side, Alex prepared himself for the challenges ahead, ready to fight for his ambitions and dreams.

Chapter 6: Eve's Introduction

Alex walked through the bustling streets, the sun hanging low in the sky, casting long shadows on the pavement. The air felt electric, charged with potential and mystery. It was a typical day, yet everything changed when Alex crossed paths with Eve Sinclair. She stood by a coffee shop, her laptop open on the table in front of her. Her brow was furrowed in concentration, and her fingers danced across the keys as if she were in a race against time.

Eve was no ordinary person. She was an expert in artificial intelligence, known for her groundbreaking studies in the field. Her passion for decoding complex algorithms was evident in the way she immersed herself in her work. Alex had heard about her through the grapevine, how she had been cracking some of the toughest codes that baffled even the best minds in the industry. But today, it was not just AI that had brought them together; it was the encrypted messages that had captured both their attentions.

Without much hesitation, Alex approached her table. "Excuse me, are you Eve Sinclair?" he asked, his voice a mix of curiosity and urgency. She looked up, her eyes widening slightly in recognition. She nodded, gesturing for him to sit down.

"I've been waiting for someone to show up," she said, her tone both inviting and cautious. "I've been receiving some strange messages, and I think they're connected to you."

Alex felt a shiver of excitement. He could hardly believe his luck. He explained briefly that he had been working on the encrypted messages for weeks and that they seemed to point to a larger puzzle, one that was still unfolding. Eve listened carefully, her interest piqued as he recounted his experiences. The two quickly discovered that they shared a common goal.

The Fragile Alliance

As they exchanged information, a fragile alliance began to form between them. They had both been receiving bits and pieces of similar encrypted messages. Each message felt like a breadcrumb, leading them deeper into a realm of mystery and intrigue. It became clear that neither of them could uncover the truth on their own. They needed each other's skills and insights.

Alex brought a unique perspective to the table. He had spent years studying the underlying patterns of the messages. He could recognize repeated sequences and anomalies that others might overlook. Eve, with her technical know-how, could decipher the more complex elements of the code. Together, they made a perfect team, blending Alex's analytical skills with Eve's technological prowess.

To kick off their collaboration, they decided to analyze the encrypted messages they had received separately. They set up a timeline to track every interaction and each new piece of information. As they worked, they realized that many of the messages were formatted in a way that hinted at a larger framework, like pieces of a puzzle waiting to be assembled.

Eve suggested they create a visual map, which could help them see the connections more clearly. She pulled out a large sheet of paper and began to draw. Alex watched as she sketched out the different elements of the messages, noting down the key themes and unusual phrases that kept appearing. It was fascinating to see how the pieces slowly came together.

Building the Framework

"Each of these messages has a pattern," Alex said, pointing to the paper. "Look at how certain words are repeated. They might signify something important."

Eve nodded, her eyes gleaming with realization. "You're right. This could be a code within a code. We need to break it down further." They worked late into the night, fueled by caffeine and determination. Each hour brought them closer to understanding the hidden meanings behind the encrypted letters.

As days turned into weeks, their bond grew stronger. They met regularly, often in the same coffee shop where they had first connected. With each gathering, they shared more than just ideas; they exchanged stories about their lives and aspirations. Alex learned about Eve's journey into the world of artificial intelligence, a field she had always been passionate about since childhood. She told him how she had built her first robot when she was just ten years old, a toy that responded to simple commands.

In turn, Alex shared his experiences in coding and how he had stumbled upon the encrypted messages while investigating a mystery from his past. Their conversation painted a vivid picture of two individuals driven by curiosity and a desire for understanding. They were both unconventional in their ways, bold in pursuing the answers that eluded so many.

Decoding the Messages

With a solid understanding of each other's strengths, they began an intensive phase of their investigation. The encrypted messages were more than just jumbled letters. They contained references to various sources, including news articles, scientific papers, and even social media posts.

Eve developed a method for categorizing these references, allowing them to investigate the significance of each one. She taught Alex how to use certain software to filter through vast amounts of data. Together, they analyzed each reference, cross-referencing them to discover if there was a broader narrative at play. Their days flowed into nights filled with deep discussions and brainstorming sessions.

As they deciphered the messages, they stumbled upon a particular phrase that stood out: "The future is coded." It felt more than just a random string of words. It was as if there was an underlying prophecy embedded within the messages. They decided to research the phrase, leading them down various rabbit holes.

Alex found references to it in literature, while Eve discovered its mention in a tech seminar notes she had once attended. As pieces of the puzzle started fitting together, they realized that the messages might relate to a groundbreaking project in artificial intelligence—a project that could alter the future of technology.

Facing Challenges Together

Yet, as excitement built over their discoveries, they faced challenges. There were moments of frustration and confusion when the messages led them astray or didn't connect. They encountered dead ends, and doubt loomed in the back of their minds.

During one such moment, Alex leaned back in his chair, rubbing his eyes. "Maybe we're not supposed to figure this out," he said with a sigh. Eve, sensing the gravity of his words, reached across the table and placed her hand atop his.

"Don't say that," she replied with conviction. "We'll find a way. Just remember the goal we shared. There's something bigger at play here." Her optimism sparked renewed determination within Alex. They would not give up. They would push through the obstacles together.

The partnership between Alex and Eve blossomed under these stresses. They learned to navigate each other's frustrations and weaknesses while celebrating each victory, no matter how small. Every coded message they understood felt like a triumph ringing in their ears, propelling them forward.

Together, they were not just chasing after a mystery; they were weaving their destiny. The challenge complicated their lives, yet it enriched them in ways they didn't expect. As they grew closer, the fragile alliance transformed into a partnership grounded in trust and shared ambition.

Their journey had only just begun, and the world of codes and mysteries lay ahead, ripe for exploration. Through every encrypted message, every hour spent together, Alex and Eve would continue to unlock the door to the secrets that lay waiting, hidden just beneath the surface.

Chapter 7: The Data Breach

A massive data breach rattled the walls of a major tech corporation. News spread quickly, sending waves of panic through employees and stakeholders alike. The company had been a leader in technological innovation, and now they found themselves at the center of an immense security crisis. Customers were rightly concerned about the safety of their personal information, and the governors of the corporation engaged in urgent meetings to assess the damage. This situation was not just about lost data; it was also about trust. Alex, a dedicated software engineer, worked long hours developing the latest encryption system for the corporation. However, as he heard more about the breach, he couldn't shake off an unsettling feeling. Was there a connection between the encryption he was working on and the breach undermining the corporation's reputation?

In the moments of confusion and chaos, Eve, a seasoned expert in artificial intelligence, found herself at the forefront of discussions. Her experience and insight were invaluable, especially in a crisis like this. As she analyzed the situation, she pointed out how advanced AI systems might play a role in data security. The more Alex listened to her, the more he realized that understanding the intersection between AI and cybersecurity was crucial. AI systems could potentially enhance security protocols, but they could also introduce vulnerabilities if not properly managed. Eve made it clear that every piece of technology had its strengths and weaknesses, and it was important to address those in the wake of such an alarming incident.

As Alex delved deeper into his work, he began to investigate the encryption methods he had been using. His focus shifted from mere functionality to the underlying algorithm and any potential weaknesses it might harbor. He knew that encryption was meant to safeguard data by transforming it into a format that could not be read without a specific key. However, Alex also understood that if hackers had found a way to bypass those protections, the consequences would be dire. He dug into various encryption standards like AES (Advanced Encryption Standard) and RSA (Rivest-Shamir-Adleman) to see if they could provide insights on how to strengthen his current approach.

Through his research, Alex learned that even the most robust encryption methods could be compromised if the keys were not stored securely. He stressed the importance of key management systems in ensuring that the encrypted data remained safe. For instance, he noted that using a hardware security module (HSM) could provide an extra layer of protection. HSMs are physical devices designed to manage digital keys securely and perform cryptographic operations. By employing such systems, Alex learned how organizations could better safeguard sensitive information from potential breaches. He pondered over the possibility that if the major tech corporation had implemented a more rigorous key management system, perhaps they could have prevented the breach altogether.

Meanwhile, Eve continued to highlight the role AI could play in identifying potential security threats. She explained that AI systems could analyze vast amounts of data to detect irregular behaviors that might indicate a breach is underway. For example, if an AI system monitored network traffic and noticed an unusual spike in data transfer, it could trigger an automatic alert. By employing machine learning algorithms, the company could train AI to distinguish normal activity from suspicious patterns, enabling faster responses to potential threats. It became increasingly evident to Alex that leveraging AI could play a crucial role in the corporation's future security strategies.

Eve also introduced the idea of incorporating predictive analytics within the corporation's data security framework. Predictive analytics is a method that utilizes historical data, machine learning, and statistical algorithms to forecast future outcomes. In this scenario, the company could analyze past breaches and vulnerabilities to predict potential weaknesses in their systems. For instance, if a certain software component had been exploited frequently in other companies, the corporation could prioritize securing that component. Alex felt a growing eagerness to collaborate with Eve and others in utilizing these innovative approaches to strengthen their defenses.

As the days passed, the tech corporation worked tirelessly to rectify the situation. Meetings were held frequently to discuss plans on how to recover from the breach and prevent future occurrences. Alex and his team focused on refining their encryption methods while integrating Eve's recommendations for AI-enhanced security. Collaboration became the cornerstone of their efforts, as team members willingly shared insights and explored various solutions to improve their overall security posture. Everyone recognized that rebuilding trust required not only technical solutions but also transparent communication with clients and stakeholders.

One day, while reflecting on his findings, Alex decided to hold a training session for his colleagues. He wanted to share the knowledge he had gathered about encryption and AI and inspire others to think critically about data security. He prepared a presentation that covered the fundamentals of encryption, proper key management practices, and the advantages of using AI for predictive analytics. The session was well-received, and participants engaged in lively discussions. Alex was thrilled to see that his peers were excited about enhancing their security measures, and he felt a renewed sense of purpose.

As the corporation faced the aftermath, discussions around regulations and industry standards also surfaced. Over the years, regulations like GDPR (General Data Protection Regulation) and CCPA (California Consumer Privacy Act) have been implemented to protect consumer data. Alex and his team recognized that adherence to these regulations was no longer optional; it was a necessity. They committed to ensuring that all their processes aligned with these standards, which would not only help them regain customer trust but also ensure long-term compliance in the evolving digital landscape.

In the following weeks, Alex witnessed how the crisis instigated a culture shift within the corporation. Employees began to understand the importance of cybersecurity in everyday operations. They started to prioritize security in their design processes, developing applications with security as the primary focus from the outset. The mindset changed from reactive to proactive, making security a fundamental aspect of their work. Alex felt proud to be part of a team that was pioneering such transformations, especially in an industry where data breaches had become alarmingly common.

As discussions about the breach continued, speculation arose regarding the source of the attack. Some suggested that it may have originated from a competitor looking to undermine the corporation's reputation. Others believed that it was a sophisticated attack from an external criminal organization. Alex recognized the importance of decisive action as they worked to mitigate the impact of the breach. This included gathering forensic evidence, conducting audits, and reviewing all current security protocols. Understanding the threat landscape, they understood that knowledge was power, and the more they knew, the better prepared they would be for future incidents.

Through this experience, the corporation learned invaluable lessons that would shape its future. Security was no longer viewed as merely an IT issue; it became a collective responsibility shared across all departments. Alex and Eve continued to push for innovation, conducting research projects to explore new technologies and methodologies. This incident had underscored the need for stronger defenses, and they were committed to ensuring that their systems would be a fortress against future attacks. They wanted to trust their technology, knowing it was built on a foundation of rigorous security practices.

As the chapter unfolded, it became clear that the journey toward strong cybersecurity was ongoing. Alex was determined to stay on the cutting edge, learning and adapting to the ever-evolving threats. Eve remained a crucial ally, encouraging collaboration and communication among teams. There was a sense of unity as they moved forward together. The lessons learned from the data breach would not only guide their recovery process but also inspire a renewed commitment to excellence in data security for the future.

Chapter 8: The Order

Alex and Eve stumbled upon a secretive group called "The Order." Initially, they viewed it just as a rumor, one of those whispers that float around in dark corners of the internet. But as they dug deeper into the origins of the encrypted message they found, they realized that The Order was more than just a myth. This group appeared to be orchestrating events on a global scale. With hidden algorithms at their disposal, The Order seemed to have an influence that reached far beyond what anyone had imagined.

The Order is said to be manipulating various systems across the globe. To understand this, one must first grasp what a secretive organization is. Such groups often work behind closed doors, making decisions that affect millions without any public knowledge. They operate in the shadows, keeping their intentions and methods concealed. In the case of The Order, there are claims that their reach extends into every significant pillar of society, from the economy to political systems.

For example, consider how economies function through intricate systems. When Alex and Eve learned about how The Order was believed to influence financial markets, they started looking into how algorithms could impact stock prices. Algorithms are sets of instructions that computers follow to perform tasks. In the financial world, they help determine buying and selling processes. If a group has control over such algorithms, they can effectively sway market behavior. This raises questions about fairness and transparency. If an unseen group is pulling the strings, can any financial system truly be trusted?

In addition to economics, The Order supposedly plays a role in global politics. Political agendas are often shaped by the flow of information. If The Order can control what information is disseminated to the public, they could sway public opinion and thus influence elections. Alex and Eve discovered articles pointing to instances where media coverage was manipulated to favor certain political candidates. For instance, when a major news outlet decides to spotlight specific issues while downplaying others, it creates a narrative that can heavily influence voters.

The first step Alex and Eve took was to explore the origins of this encrypted message. They believed that by tracing its roots, they might uncover connections to The Order. They spent nights researching on various forums, using search engines to their advantage. They followed threads that discussed The Order, finding pieces of information that seemed to fit together like a puzzle. They would often jot down notes, creating diagrams showcasing their findings.

They realized that many discussions surrounding The Order often pointed to high-profile individuals in government and finance. Through social media discussions and blog posts, they began to see correlations between key decision-makers and suspicious actions surrounding economic fluctuations. This investigation opened their eyes to the potential for corruption and deceit in systems they once believed were stable.

As they delved deeper, Alex and Eve learned the importance of being critical of the sources they encountered. Many claimed to have inside knowledge about The Order, but they lacked credibility. They came across countless conspiracy theories that spoke of hidden meetings and coded messages. The key was discerning which information was reliable and which was fuel for sensationalism. They developed a checklist to assess sources: was the author credible, did they provide evidence, and was their motivation behind sharing the information clear?

After gathering enough information about The Order, it became apparent that they needed a plan. They wanted to unravel the layers of secrecy surrounding this group and share their findings with the world. They decided to create a blog dedicated to their research. This would allow them to document their journey and provide a space for others who were interested in the same topic.

They started writing entries detailing their discoveries. Each post was structured like a chapter, beginning with an overview of what they learned that week. They included links to articles they found useful, incorporating factual data for context. It was essential to them that their readers had access to the same resources they used. They believed that knowledge should be shared, especially when it came to topics that affect society.

In crafting their blog, Alex and Eve found that they not only wanted to report on The Order but also raise awareness regarding the implications of such a group. They wanted their readers to grasp the seriousness of being informed about the systems that govern society. They included actionable steps for individuals to take, such as researching the origins of news stories or questioning information presented to them.

For instance, they wanted to encourage everyone to think critically about political advertisements. Often, these advertisements do not tell the whole story. They can manipulate emotions to gain support for a specific candidate, leaving out important facts that should be considered. Alex and Eve suggested that readers examine multiple sources when evaluating political candidates and their policies.

As their blog gained traction, they also began reaching out to others who shared their concerns. They posted on forums where people discussed similar topics, inviting dialogue and collaboration. This broadened their network and provided them with more insights into The Order. They realized that they were not alone in wanting to shed light on this mysterious group.

Among their contacts, they discovered a former journalist who had investigated financial algorithms for years. This contact was eager to share their research and findings with Alex and Eve. They set up a call, and the conversation opened their minds to even more possibilities regarding The Order's machinations. The journalist explained how certain hedge funds used algorithms not just for profit but also to influence markets, manipulating stocks to their advantage with no regard for everyday investors.

With each new piece of information, Alex and Eve felt a mix of excitement and trepidation. They were on the path of uncovering something significant, but what if the influence of The Order was so extensive that exposing them could have dangerous repercussions? They weighed their options carefully, discussing the risks and rewards of bringing this information to light. Should they continue to work in the shadows, or was it time to come forward?

Through late-night discussions and relentless research, Alex and Eve became determined to expose the truth. The thrill of discovery invigorated them, but they knew they had to proceed carefully. There was still a long way to go in unraveling the complexities surrounding The Order, and they were just getting started. Their journey was filled with uncertainty, but they were driven by a shared purpose: to shine a light on the darkness and reveal the forces that sought to manipulate the world around them.

Chapter 9: Cipher's Betrayal

Alex and Eve had been working tirelessly for weeks. They had finally started to make progress in their quest to uncover the truth behind the secretive organization known as The Order. Every late night spent pouring over files, every conversation with hesitant informants, and every street corner rendezvous felt like it was leading them somewhere important. Alex and Eve were beginning to feel a sense of hope, a belief that they could succeed. They were a team, relying on each other to navigate the dangers around them. Trust was everything in their line of work, and they had placed their trust in Cipher, their trusted informant.

Cipher had always been a wild card in their plans. He was known for his quick wit and the way he always seemed to be one step ahead. He provided them with crucial tips about The Order, and they thought they could count on him. Alex often felt a mix of admiration and caution when it came to Cipher. He was unpredictable, but he had a knack for finding information that others could not. He knew the underbelly of the city like the back of his hand. It was hard not to appreciate his abilities, but Alex also knew that trust was hard-earned and could be quickly lost.

One evening, as they sat in a dimly lit café, Alex and Eve shared their recently gleaned insights. They laughed over odds-and-ends, discussing their plans for the next steps. Eve had a great idea about how to lure out one of The Order's key members, and Alex could see the light in her eyes as she spoke. But as they were in the middle of the conversation, the café door opened with a creak. Cipher walked in, and a chill washed over the table. His entire demeanor had shifted. Gone was the playful interloper; instead, he appeared serious, almost burdened. Alex could sense something unsettling in the air.

Cipher approached their table but held back for a moment. There was a look on his face Alex had never seen before. It was not the usual glint of mischief but rather a stormy mix of guilt and determination. Alex felt a lump in his throat, unsure of what would come out of Cipher's mouth next. He could recall moments when Cipher had dodged questions or misled them, playing the role of the enigmatic informant, but this felt different. This felt like a reckoning was about to unfold.

With a heavy pause, Cipher finally spoke. "I have to tell you both something important," he said, the weight of his words hanging in the air. His tone was unlike anything they had experienced before, drawing the attention of nearby patrons. "I made a deal," he continued, looking only at the tabletop. "I gave The Order information about you. In return, they promised protection for me." The gravity of his confession hit Alex like a punch to the gut. Betrayal hung heavily in the air, wrapping around them like a thick fog. Alex's heart raced. How could Cipher do this to them?

Eve's expression shifted from confusion to frustration, her eyes narrowing. "How could you sell us out? We trusted you!" She leaned forward, her voice rising just above the ambient noise of the café. Cipher looked up, and Alex could see the regret etched into his features. "You don't understand. They were going to kill me," he pleaded, desperation creeping into his voice. "I didn't have a choice!"

The café, once a comforting place for them, transformed into a battleground of emotions. Alex felt betrayed, lost in a whirlwind of disappointment and anger. They had fought their way through so many obstacles together, only to have their ally turn against them. He struggled to find words; every thought felt jumbled in his head. "What information did you give them?" he finally managed to ask.

Cipher hesitated before speaking again. "They know about your plans, about everything you've been working on," he admitted. Alex's mind raced as he tried to absorb this new reality. They had worked for so long to stay under the radar, but now it felt as though their safety net was ripped away. "What happens now?" Eve asked, her voice trembling with a mix of fear and disbelief.

Cipher's shoulders slumped as he spoke, "I don't know, but we have to move fast. They will come after you both." The talk of urgency mingled with the betrayal, creating a confusing web of emotions. Alex could see the panic in Eve's eyes, mirroring his own sense of dread. With Cipher's revelation, the shifts on the chessboard had changed dramatically; they were no longer the players but had become the pawns fighting to survive.

They exited the café, the chill of the night air hitting them hard. The shadows felt longer, and every noise made their hearts race. Initially, they had expected to walk away with new plans and strategic advantages, but now an unsettling sense of vulnerability enveloped them. Cipher urged them to find a safe place, but Alex wrestled with the reality of having once viewed Cipher as an ally. There was little time to dwell on disappointments; they had to act fast.

As they stumbled into a quiet alley, Alex turned to Cipher, "Is it possible to undo this?" The words slipped out before he could stop himself. Cipher shook his head and looked like a man carrying a heavy burden. "Once you betray someone, you can't take it back. You can only run and find a way to protect yourself." Alex felt anger swell back inside him. Was this the same man who had once guided them?

Eve, holding her breath, grabbed Alex's arm. "We need a plan," she said firmly. But whatever confidence she had sounded fragile. The flickering street lights painted their faces in alternating spots of light and dark, reflecting the chaos of their emotions. They had felt a rush of adrenaline in the past, but it seemed as if their trust had been flipped into an unexpected reality—distrust. Cipher had put a wedge between them, and they now stood on different sides.

Throughout the night, ideas raced through Alex's mind. Could they find a way to leverage the very information Cipher had given? In desperation, he began brainstorming counter-strategies. Even if Cipher had betrayed them, he might have inadvertently provided the very detail they needed to regain the advantage. "What if we turn the tables?" he suggested. Eve looked at him, intrigued yet hesitant. She grasped the potential but grappled with the fallout of having Cipher as part of their plan.

Cipher stayed silent, his expression unreadable. The tension was palpable as Alex and Eve shared quick, silent glances, weighing their options. This could be the moment where they transformed a setback into an advantage, but it was laced with uncertainty. Betrayal had changed everything they knew, and even as they plotted their next moves, doubt lingered in the air like the distant hum of sirens.

They ventured deeper into the night, unsure of where this path would lead. Every shadow felt like a watchful eye, and worry crept back into Alex's mind. Cipher had become unpredictable. There was no telling how far he might go to protect himself. Despite the unsettling feelings, they had to regroup and figure out their next steps. What could they do to shield themselves from the fallout of Cipher's choices? The night seemed endless, and the upcoming confrontation with The Order loomed like a storm on the horizon, threatening to engulf them all.

Chapter 10: Into the Dark Web

With nowhere else to turn, Alex and Eve find themselves drawn into the shadowy world of the dark web. This is not a place they ever wanted to enter, but their desperation drives them. The traditional ways of gathering information have failed them, and they know that the dark web holds secrets that could change everything. They sit together, surrounded by their computer screens, knowing they must tread carefully.

Exploring the dark web is no simple task. It requires special tools and knowledge to navigate the hidden corners of the Internet. Alex installs a secure browser called Tor, which helps them access sites that are not indexed by traditional search engines. They both feel a mixture of excitement and fear as they prepare to delve into this unknown territory. It is essential that they keep their identities safe while on this journey, so they take extra precautions, using encrypted messaging and virtual private networks.

Once they are connected, they come across various forums where users share information about underground activities. Alex and Eve sift through countless posts, searching for anything that might relate to The Order. They stumble upon a thread discussing various groups operating in the dark web. Some members talk about hacking incidents and their connections to large corporations. Others mention mysterious networks that are rumored to influence the digital economy.

As they dive deeper, they come across disturbing evidence that points to The Order's operations. They discover plans for total control through sophisticated digital systems. This plan involves implementing systems that monitor people's digital footprints, collecting data on their activities, and even predicting their future actions. It becomes increasingly clear that The Order seeks to create an environment where privacy is a thing of the past. Alex and Eve realize they must act quickly to expose these plans before it is too late.

They find a document that outlines a roadmap for achieving this control. It details the steps The Order plans to take, including infiltrating governments and large tech companies. This document reveals a manipulative strategy to create dependency on digital systems, effectively making people rely on them for every aspect of their lives. As Alex reads the details, he feels his stomach churn. They understand that if these plans come to fruition, people's freedom will be in serious jeopardy.

In another chat room, they encounter individuals discussing a recent breach of a government system. The leaked conversations are filled with anxiety about The Order's influence. Some even express regret about their naivete, realizing too late that their data was being harvested without their knowledge. Alex and Eve take notes, knowing these conversations can provide invaluable insights into how The Order operates. They see how people unwittingly give up pieces of themselves, believing they are safe, when in reality, they are merely feeding the machine.

Throughout this exploration, Alex and Eve constantly remind themselves to stay focused. They talk to each other, sharing what they find, piecing together a larger picture. They understand that it is not enough to uncover information; they must also plan a way to share it with the public. The potential dangers are real, and they know the risks involved in publishing sensitive information could put them in jeopardy.

As they progress, they meet other users on the dark web. Some are hackers who want to take a stand against The Order, while others are just curious individuals searching for truth. Alex and Eve realize they can't fight this battle alone. They engage with these users, discussing their findings and hearing stories of how The Order has affected different communities. The shared frustration leads to a motivation to unite against a common enemy.

Through their conversations, they learn about digital security measures that can help protect them and others. They discover about encryption, secure communication tools, and ways to stay anonymous online. Knowledge becomes a powerful weapon in their arsenal against The Order, and they make it their mission to share this information as widely as possible. They begin drafting a plan for how to approach this fight, outlining steps they can take to mobilize and gather more support.

Their research takes them into the depths of the dark web, encountering challenges that test their resolve. They come across disinformation campaigns designed to mislead people about The Order. Recognizing these tactics is essential, as they learn that the battle of information is just as critical as any physical fight against oppression. The dark web becomes a learning ground, helping them develop strategies for navigating misinformation.

Soon, they uncover a network of dissidents who are already working to counter The Order's influence. This underground community shares vital resources, strategies, and connections that help them amplify their efforts. Alex and Eve join discussions with these individuals, sharing what they have learned and hearing first-hand accounts of The Order's reach. They find allies who are willing to support their mission. These connections inspire Alex and Eve, reinforcing the idea that they are not alone in this fight.

Each piece of information they gather builds momentum towards a larger understanding of The Order's plans. They document everything, creating a detailed report that outlines the connections, strategies, and implications of their findings. They know this could be a crucial piece of intelligence that shines light on a dark reality.

As they prepare to take their findings public, they face a critical crossroads. The dark web is dangerous, and exposing the truth could have dire consequences. But Alex and Eve feel a sense of urgency; knowledge is powerful, and people need to be aware of the dangers posed by The Order. They remind each other not to lose hope, emphasizing that even in the darkest of places, there's the potential for change.

Together, they craft a message, balancing urgency with caution. They decide to use secure channels to reach out to trusted journalists who specialize in investigative reporting. The importance of this step cannot be overstated; getting the information into the right hands could mobilize a broader response, igniting public interest and initiating change.

With their research and connections from the dark web in hand, Alex and Eve prepare to face the challenges ahead, knowing they are embarking on a journey that will demand their full commitment. They realize that this moment is just the beginning. Their resolve strengthens as they step away from the screens, ready to tackle whatever comes next in the fight against The Order.

Chapter 11: The Algorithm

Alex sat in his dimly lit room, staring intently at his computer screen. The lines of code scrolled past quickly, but one section caught his attention. It was a part of a message that he had been working to decrypt for days. As he focused, the complexity of the algorithm began to unravel before him. With each passing moment, the pieces fell into place, revealing a highly sophisticated algorithm designed specifically to manipulate global financial markets.

This algorithm was unlike anything Alex had ever seen. It was not merely a collection of numbers or code; it was a powerful tool that, if wielded improperly, could lead to devastating consequences for economies around the world. He quickly realized the weight of what he had discovered. If this information were to fall into the wrong hands—those of a hacker or an unscrupulous organization—an economic catastrophe could ensue, affecting millions of people.

Understanding the urgency of the situation, Alex felt a surge of determination. He needed to find a way to prevent this code from being unleashed into the world. But first, he had to comprehend its full capabilities. He began to analyze its functions, breaking each component down to understand how it could be utilized to manipulate market trends.

The algorithm had several layers of complexity. At its core, it contained various mathematical formulas that calculated vast amounts of data from different financial sectors. This enabled it to predict market shifts with a high degree of accuracy. For instance, if the algorithm detected a sudden drop in the stock prices of key companies, it could execute trades to profit from this downturn, essentially turning a crisis into an opportunity for financial gain.

As Alex dug deeper, he noticed how the algorithm could also exploit weaknesses in trading systems. For example, if there was a flaw in a bank's trading software, the algorithm could bypass the security measures, gaining unfettered access to sensitive financial information. It could execute trades before humans even had a chance to react, capitalizing on the element of speed that the digital world provided.

This realization sent chills down Alex's spine. Not only could it manipulate stocks, but it could also affect currencies, commodities, and even cryptocurrencies. The global financial network was intertwined, and a manipulation in one area could trigger rippling effects across various markets. An economic disaster could unfold in a matter of hours, affecting everything from small businesses to international corporations.

As he considered the potential ramifications, Alex couldn't help but think about those who might seek to misuse this algorithm. Cybercriminals, extremist groups, or even rogue state actors could potentially employ this code to wreak havoc. This raised a pressing question: who had created this algorithm? Alex needed to find out more about its origin.

With a newfound sense of urgency, he began to trace the origins of the message containing the algorithm. He thought about the different individuals and organizations he had encountered throughout his investigation. Each one could hold a piece of the puzzle. Even seemingly innocuous characters might have valuable information about who could be behind such a dangerous creation.

Alex made a list of potential contacts. There were hackers he had met during his investigation who had invaluable insights into coding and cybersecurity. There were also financial experts who understood market dynamics better than anyone else. By reaching out to these individuals, he hoped to gather more information about the algorithm and its creators.

He decided to start with an old friend—a cybersecurity expert named Tara. They had worked together on various projects in the past, and Alex trusted her instincts. He sent her a secure message, explaining the details about the algorithm and its possible implications. He asked if she could spare some time to discuss it further. Within moments, he received a reply, indicating Tara was intrigued and eager to meet.

The next day, they met at a coffee shop that offered a secluded corner for discussions. In hushed tones, Alex explained the intricacies of the algorithm. Tara's eyes widened with each detail he shared. She understood immediately the potential threats it posed. They talked extensively about how to track down its creators and what steps to take to contain the algorithm's reach.

Tara suggested a few strategies for analyzing digital footprints. They decided to delve into the dark web, a place often associated with illegal activities and hacking. It was a risky endeavor, but it might offer clues about who was behind the algorithm. Alex felt a mix of excitement and trepidation as they planned out their next steps.

As they boarded their mission, he pondered about the risks involved. Not only were they dealing with a dangerous algorithm, but they could also be stepping into a world filled with unpredictable individuals. The world of hacking had its complexities, and the players involved were not to be underestimated.

With a clear plan, they began their investigation. They dug through online forums, seeking discussions that might reference the algorithm. It was fascinating to see how people communicated in coded language, sharing knowledge while attempting to evade law enforcement. Alex felt the thrill of being part of a digital treasure hunt, each clue bringing him closer to the truth.

After hours of sifting through information, they stumbled upon a promising lead. A user on a dark web forum had mentioned an upcoming gathering of hackers. This event could potentially include those who had worked on or at least had knowledge of the algorithm. Excited yet nervous, Alex and Tara decided they had to attend this gathering to gather more intel.

As the date approached, they prepared for the event. They knew they would have to tread carefully. Approaching strangers in a place where trust was scarce would require strategy. Alex crafted a persona that would allow him to blend in with the tech-savvy crowd without drawing unwanted attention.

When the day arrived, Alex's heart raced as they entered the dimly lit venue filled with murmuring groups. There were screens displaying complex code and a buzz in the air like an electric charge. He looked around, feeling the weight of the algorithm still heavy on his mind. Finding the right people to approach would be crucial. Patience and observation would be key.

They began to circulate, engaging in casual conversations, absorbing the atmosphere. Soon, Alex caught wind of a small group gathered around a table, discussing a recent hacking incident that had rocked the financial sector. This could be a goldmine of information. With Tara by his side, Alex approached the group, ready to listen closely and seize any opportunity to learn about the algorithm and its creators.

Chapter 12: A New Enemy

A mysterious figure emerges in the shadows, known only as "Shade." This person has a reputation for being cunning and elusive. Shade is not just an ordinary foe; they possess a wealth of resources and advanced technology that make them a formidable opponent. With each passing day, it becomes increasingly clear that Shade has a plan that involves Alex and Eve. The two friends find themselves caught up in a dangerous game, and they must navigate the challenges that arise from this new threat.

Alex and Eve start to notice unusual occurrences around them. Things go missing, and every time they believe they are safe, something else happens. Shade seems to anticipate their moves, almost as if they are always one step ahead. For instance, when Alex decides to take an alternate route home after school, a strange vehicle follows them for a while. Eve notices this and suggests they take a different path altogether.

Eve becomes more concerned as the days go by. She suggests that they need to gather information about Shade. They begin by reaching out to old contacts and friends, hoping to uncover any leads. Together, they compile a list of potential resources that could help them in their search. They decide to meet each informant in a public place, ensuring their safety.

Through their investigation, they meet a former tech expert who has dealt with similar threats in the past. This expert advises them to look for patterns in Shade's behavior. They learn that Shade often targets those who are close to their main objective, manipulating their surroundings, and using technology to create distractions. This information prompts Alex and Eve to devise a plan to protect themselves.

As they dig deeper, they discover that Shade's technology is more advanced than they initially thought. It involves drones and surveillance equipment that can track movements and gather information from afar. The realization hits them hard: they can't let Shade control their lives. It means they need to be clever about their next steps. They decide to use some smaller tech of their own to fight back against this invasive presence.

They explore various self-defense options to stay safe. Alex researches affordable gadgets, while Eve practices their communication skills, ensuring they are always in touch. They find it helpful to use code words in their messages, just in case Shade is monitoring their conversations. They know they must outsmart this enemy.

Eve proposes that they create decoys to confuse Shade. They start to think creatively about how they can use distractions to lead Shade astray. For example, they agree to spend time at multiple locations in their town on the same day, essentially splitting up their routine. They communicate their whereabouts constantly, making sure they can adjust plans if necessary.

Meanwhile, Shade makes their move. Alex and Eve encounter strange obstacles that seem directed at them. They face glitches in their devices and unexpected changes in their schedules that push them outside their comfort zones. It is frustrating, and their patience begins to wear thin. They must remind each other to stay calm and focused so they don't fall into any traps.

Throughout these tense moments, their communication with each other grows even stronger. They learn to rely on their instincts, which helps them navigate through the difficulties they encounter. They engage in brainstorming sessions to improve their strategy, all while remaining aware of their surroundings. They understand that they must act smart and not let fear dictate their actions.

While they adapt to the pressure of their new reality, they also take time to enjoy their friendship amid the chaos. Alex and Eve remind each other to do ordinary things, like watching movies or hanging out with friends. This helps maintain a sense of normalcy in their lives, despite the external turmoil. They reflect on their journey and how their friendship has gotten them through tough times before, which strengthens their resolve.

As they learn more about Shade's tactics, they come to understand that this enemy feeds off their fear and confusion. This realization empowers them. They shift their mindset from merely reacting to Shade's moves to being proactive about their own safety. They start to take calculated risks, knowing that they can mitigate harm by staying united.

On one of their outings, they overhear a conversation about a shadow organization that Shade is apparently connected with. This leads them to explore the idea of gathering more intelligence about this group. They decide to research any information they can find online and speak to others who might have encountered similar threats. Caution becomes their guiding principle, as they know the risks involved in digging deeper.

The mounting pressure brings new tensions into their relationship, as each one deals with their fear in different ways. Eve channels her anxiety into action, while Alex sometimes hesitates to move forward. They both realize this and agree to openly discuss their feelings. This openness helps strengthen their bond and keeps them focused on the mission at hand. They realize that trust and communication are vital in overcoming Shade's schemes.

They dive into learning more about the technology they might use to counteract Shade's advantages. They seek out workshops and tutorials online, teaching themselves useful skills. It is fascinating to them as they uncover more about how the tools work. Their determination to learn gives them new strategies to put into practice.

As they prepare for what lies ahead, they know it is essential to have a backup plan. Alex and Eve outline all their strategies on a whiteboard, establishing steps for both cautious maneuvers and bold actions. They assign specific roles to keep things organized, ensuring each of them knows what to do in a crisis.

Their preparations begin to pay off. They become more adept at recognizing Shade's tactics and adjusting their plans in real-time. They strategize around Shade's expected moves, staying vigilant and ready. Their commitment strengthens, and they begin to feel a sense of power as they gain control over their situation. They no longer see themselves as victims; instead, they are warriors facing a new battle.

One night, they decide to implement a surprise tactic in one of their outings. By using all they have learned, they manage to gain the upper hand, at least momentarily. This gives them the confidence to continue pushing back against Shade. The emotional high from this victory fuels their determination, providing a much-needed boost of energy.

The more they confront Shade's relentless pursuit, the more they learn about themselves. They understand the value of their friendship and realize they are more resilient together. When they face adversity, they can lean on each other for support. This newfound strength becomes a source of empowerment, reminding them that they are never truly alone in their fight.

As they continue their battle against the mysterious Shade, they understand that this is not just about survival but about reclaiming their lives. It is a journey for them, full of twists and turns, as they discover new strengths within themselves. Each day brings new possibilities and challenges, and they remind themselves that they have the tools to stand against their new enemy.

Chapter 13: The First Battle

Alex and Eve stood outside the sprawling glass building that housed the headquarters of The Order. The sun was setting, casting a warm golden hue on the structure, but there was nothing warm about their mission. They were about to launch their first offensive against a group notorious for its financial manipulation and illicit dealings. The stakes were high, and the air buzzed with tension as they prepared to disrupt The Order's shady financial operations.

Gathering their gear, Alex looked at Eve and said, "Are you ready for this?" Eve simply nodded, determination in her eyes. They had been planning this operation for weeks, analyzing data and gathering intel on the financial methods employed by The Order. It was imperative for them to strike when the time was right. This was not just a mission; it was a chance to expose the corrupt tactics that had been hidden from the public eye.

Before they approached, they reviewed their plan. First, they would create a distraction by leaking manipulated information about The Order's upcoming financial maneuverings. Simultaneously, they would infiltrate the network to find proof of the illegal activities. The combined effort would sow confusion within The Order and buy them the time they needed to slip in unnoticed.

As they moved into position, Eve activated her smartphone to broadcast the false information. The notification spread like wildfire on social media. Screens lit up across the city as the public reacted to the news, questioning the integrity of The Order's operations. They watched with bated breath as comments and shares multiplied, each notification signaling a ripple effect that threatened to throw The Order's plans off course.

With the public's eyes now on The Order, Alex initiated the second phase of their operation. He connected to a nearby Wi-Fi network, using an application they had crafted to bypass the security layers guarding The Order's systems. The initial moments were filled with anxiety as they awaited a response to their breach. Each second felt like an eternity. But, as his screen flickered to life, he realized they had succeeded.

"Got it!" Alex whispered, revealing a trove of documents that detailed financial manipulations, illicit investments, and suspicious transactions. They could hardly believe their luck. With the data in hand, they needed to extract it quickly before they were discovered.

However, before they could fully download the information, an alarm pierced the air. The building's security had detected their presence. It was at that moment they realized the gravity of their situation. They had underestimated The Order's vigilance. Alex and Eve exchanged glances and knew they had to act fast.

"What now?" Eve asked, her voice tinged with urgency.

"We need to get out, now!" he replied. They quickly initiated their emergency protocol, and with Alex leading the way, they made a dash for the back exit. The darkness of the alley provided them some cover, but their hearts raced as they sprinted away from the building. They could hear footsteps behind them, a clear indication that Shade's operatives were hot on their tail.

Shade's operatives were well-trained and ruthless. They didn't just belong to any criminal organization; they were elite agents feared by many for their efficiency. Alex and Eve had crossed a line, and now they were being hunted. They trusted each other implicitly, knowing their survival depended on their teamwork.

As they weaved through the city's maze of streets, Alex recalled a trick he had learned from his father—a method of slipping away unnoticed. They ducked into a small café that was closing for the night, quickly concealing themselves behind an old oak table. The familiar scent of freshly brewed coffee offered a brief sense of comfort, but they had no time to relax. They peered through the window, watching for any sign of their pursuers.

Minutes felt like hours as they remained hidden. The sound of footsteps faded for a moment, but they knew it wouldn't last long. They needed a plan to escape without being caught. Eve rummaged through her bag and pulled out a small device that would disrupt nearby surveillance cameras.

"Here, we can use this to create a diversion," she suggested. Alex was impressed by her resourcefulness. They would use it to mislead their pursuers while they slipped away. They positioned themselves near an exit, their hearts pounding in unison as they prepared to activate the device.

Taking a deep breath, Eve pressed the button. In a flash, the lights flickered, and the entrance cameras went haywire. It provided the perfect distraction. They seized the moment, dashing out of the café and into the bustling streets. The cool night air filled their lungs, fueling their adrenaline as they navigated through the crowd.

They had to head towards a safe house—a location known only to them and a few trusted allies. It was a small apartment on the outskirts of the city that offered them a temporary refuge. As they moved, they exchanged brief updates on the information they gathered and how it could take down The Order. Their mission, though hindered by danger, continued to burn brightly in their minds.

Once they reached the safe house, they quickly locked the door behind them. Breathless, they slumped onto the worn couch, grateful for the temporary safety it provided. Alex glanced at Eve, who was already pouring over the data they had collected. There was so much to analyze, and they needed to turn this information into something actionable.

"I think we have enough here to expose their operations," Alex said, pointing to a series of documents that highlighted The Order's top executives and their illegal dealings. "We need to make this public."

Eve nodded, formulating a plan. "We can set up a press conference. It's risky, but if we do this right, we might just bring them down."

With their resolve strengthened and the weight of their mission pressing on them, they began to prepare. They knew that the fight against The Order was only just beginning. As they worked, the reality of their situation pressed down on them; they were in deep, and the dangers were far from over, especially with Shade's operatives on their trail.

Yet, despite the threats and uncertainty looming ahead, Alex and Eve remained steadfast in their commitment. They had taken the first step in a battle that could change everything. Their resolve would drive them forward, even when it seemed like the odds were stacked against them. The fight for justice and truth had begun.

Chapter 14: Cracking the Key

In this chapter, the characters find themselves in a tense yet exhilarating moment as they uncover a crucial key to the code that had eluded them for so long. This key is not just any ordinary piece of information; it is a vital element that opens the door to an intricate world of encryption and security protocols. The realization dawns on them that the encryption they have been dealing with is not a simple message. Instead, it serves as a backdoor into some of the most secure systems on Earth. These systems include not only government databases but also military networks that are considered fortresses of information.

The characters begin to analyze what this means for the broader picture of information security. They talk about how backdoors can be embedded within encryption to allow access to data that would normally be too secure for anyone but authorized entities. They consider various scenarios where such backdoors can act as threats and opportunities, impacting national security and personal privacy.

As they delve deeper into the mechanics of the encryption, they discuss the technical aspects of how these systems function. They explain how encryption works in general terms, for readers who may not be tech-savvy. Encryption takes plain text and transforms it into a coded version that cannot be read without a specific key. Within this framework, the backdoor acts as a hidden entry point that bypasses the usual security measures.

One of the characters suggests that they need to tread carefully. They discuss ethical implications and the moral responsibilities that come with unlocking such powerful information. Accessing government and military networks could have disastrous consequences if not handled appropriately. They debate the merits and dangers of using this information. For example, gaining insights into government operations could lead to increased transparency, but it could also expose vulnerabilities that others might exploit.

The team also brainstorms various methods to examine their findings. They think about setting up a series of tests to understand what data they can access and how deeply they can probe the system without triggering any alarms. They outline a step-by-step approach to their investigation. First, they would identify the operational parameters of the backdoor. Next, they would attempt to map out what data is available and how sensitive it is. Then, based on their findings, they would collectively decide whether to delve deeper or pull back altogether.

They should keep in mind that every action has consequences. For instance, if they reveal this backdoor to the public, they might unintentionally invite malicious actors to exploit it. Meanwhile, if they choose to keep it secret, they may be withholding information that could benefit many. The characters reflect on the weight of their responsibility and the implications of unlocking such a powerful tool.

Throughout this process, they employ a balance of caution and curiosity. As they meticulously analyze the code, they draw parallels to historical events where similar access points have been exploited. They discuss well-known incidents, such as data breaches and security leaks, and how these events shaped regulations around data protection and encryption. These real-world examples ground their technical discussion in reality, showcasing the potential consequences of their actions.

They also consider how to approach any potential whistleblowers or insiders who might possess additional knowledge about the backdoor. Leveraging contacts or networks can unlock even more information. The characters plan to conduct discreet interviews, asking targeted questions while remaining aware of the potential risks of drawing attention to themselves.

As they formulate their plan, they highlight the importance of collaboration. Each character brings their unique skills to the table, from technical knowledge to analytical thinking. They identify key roles within the project, ensuring that everyone has a hands-on approach to the investigation. The group dynamic grows as they discuss how to efficiently divide tasks while fostering creativity and problem-solving.

They explore various potential outcomes of their investigation. One scenario involves discovering unexpected alliances with other organizations that could share similar goals. This could pave the way for increased efforts in cybersecurity and information sharing among groups who want to maintain secure systems.

On the opposite end of the spectrum, they also envision risks associated with their inquiry. If they identify vulnerabilities, they know that not everyone will have good intentions. They passionately advocate for developing a set of protocols to manage both data security and personal safety. These protocols would serve as guides for their actions as they dig deeper into the systems.

In the thick of their exploration, they pause to reflect on the pervasive role of technology in everyday life. They discuss how every person today is connected in some way, whether through social media or various online services. This interconnectedness emphasizes the need for strict security measures. However, it also raises questions about privacy—how much data is too much, and who should have access to it?

The characters grow increasingly aware of the challenges they will face as they delve into military networks. They contrast the governmental systems they plan to access with their own day-to-day technology usage. They envision how the backdoor could be applied to common tools like smartphones and web applications, making it relatable to everyday users. The discussion highlights the growing tension between ensuring national security and maintaining individual freedoms.

As they wrap up their brainstorming session, there is a palpable sense of urgency in the air. All the knowledge they have uncovered and the mechanics they have unraveled press upon them the necessity to act swiftly but thoughtfully. Their mission is not just about cracking a code; it's about understanding its implications in a world dependent on technology. They mentally prepare themselves for the journey ahead, knowing that each step will be critical in navigating this new terrain.

Chapter 15: Allies and Adversaries

In this chapter, a government whistleblower steps into Alex and Eve's lives. This whistleblower reaches out to them with an offer that could potentially change the course of their mission. They present inside knowledge about The Order, a powerful group that has been the center of much intrigue and danger. The whistleblower, whose identity remains a secret at first, seeks protection in exchange for this crucial information. This sets the stage for a complex relationship. Trust is a fragile thing, especially when lives are on the line. Alex and Eve must weigh their options carefully.

Initially, the whistleblower's information seems promising. They provide detailed accounts of The Order's operations, revealing their plans and strategies. This insider knowledge includes locations of secret meetings, names of key members, and even the next targets of The Order. Alex and Eve realize that this could give them a significant advantage. They start formulating a plan based on the insights shared by the whistleblower. They understand that timing is essential in this line of work. Acting quickly could mean the difference between success and failure.

However, as they dig deeper into the whistleblower's background, they begin to uncover unsettling facts. It appears that the whistleblower may not be entirely forthright. Their motivations come into question, creating a tension-filled atmosphere. The deeper Alex and Eve examine the information, the more they realize that the whistleblower could have ulterior motives. This uncertainty adds a layer of complexity to their situation. Instead of being straightforward allies, the whistleblower becomes a potential adversary. Alex and Eve must navigate this new landscape carefully.

To address these concerns, Alex and Eve decide to put the whistleblower to the test. They devise a series of questions and situations designed to gauge his trustworthiness. This involves asking for more specific information about The Order and confirming the details he has shared with them. For example, they might ask him to detail how he came to know certain secrets or where he got his information. This process not only helps them verify the whistleblower's claims but also allows them to analyze his reactions. His body language, tone of voice, and even the way he answers can provide valuable insights into whether he is being honest.

Additionally, Alex and Eve arrange a meeting with the whistleblower in a discreet location. They choose a café with a low profile to avoid drawing any unnecessary attention. Before the meeting, they agree on a set of guidelines. They will take extra precautions to protect themselves while engaging with the whistleblower. Eve suggests bringing along a recording device—just in case they need to refer back to this crucial conversation later. This proactive approach signifies how serious they are about ensuring their safety and the success of their mission.

When the day of the meeting arrives, they feel an undercurrent of tension. The café is bustling, providing the perfect backdrop for discreet conversations. As they sit down, they can see the nervousness in the whistleblower's eyes. He appears anxious, glancing around as if he fears being watched. This reaction raises additional flags for Alex and Eve. They engage him in casual conversation before diving into the more serious matters at hand.

Throughout the discussion, they notice inconsistencies in his story. The whistleblower sometimes contradicts himself, and the details he provides often seem vague. For instance, when talking about a specific event related to The Order, he struggles to provide concrete dates or locations. His hesitation to elaborate further makes Alex and Eve exchange glances; the seeds of doubt are sprouting. They begin to understand that the stakes are even higher than they initially thought. This situation could lead to a trap rather than an opportunity.

After the meeting, Alex and Eve regroup to discuss their next steps. They reflect on the whistleblower's behavior and the information he shared. They understand that while he could be a vital asset, he might also be a double agent working for The Order. They decide to keep their plans close to their chests and not share sensitive information with the whistleblower unless absolutely necessary. This cautious strategy helps them maintain an advantage in an unpredictable situation.

As they proceed with the mission, they must also prepare for the possibility of The Order striking back. Knowing they have an insider can be both a boon and a curse. They recognize the importance of staying vigilant. Each of their moves could be anticipated by The Order if the whistleblower leaks their plans. To mitigate this risk, Alex and Eve increase their security measures and work on their escape routes.

Throughout this process, Alex and Eve continue to gather intelligence. They reach out to other contacts who may provide additional perspectives on The Order and its operations. They find that talking to various informants helps them build a more comprehensive picture of the situation. Each new piece of information helps them form strategies that keep them one step ahead of their adversaries.

Meanwhile, the whistleblower is always lingering in the back of their minds. They cannot shake off the feeling that there is more to his story than meets the eye. They devise a plan to create scenarios through which they can not only test his loyalty but also gain more insight into his character. For instance, they consider leaking false information to see if he reports it back to The Order. This type of psychological maneuvering could either expose him as an adversary or confirm his role as a reliable ally.

As the tension builds, Alex and Eve find themselves at a crossroads. They must decide how to proceed with the information they possess versus the risks posed by their new ally. Every move could lead them closer to their goals or closer to danger. This precarious balance makes their mission even more thrilling and dangerous. Choices weigh heavily on them.

In the backdrop of these developments, the character of Alex shines through. His leadership skills are on display as he navigates these complex dynamics. He often takes the lead in discussions, guiding Eve through the murky waters of trust and deception. He emphasizes the need for a careful strategy, reminding Eve that patience is key in their search for answers. Meanwhile, Eve contributes significantly with her intuition and sharp insights, ensuring that their plans remain grounded.

With the links between allies and adversaries continuously evolving, it becomes clear that relationships in this world are often multi-faceted. The lines between friend and foe blur, and the trust they placed in the whistleblower becomes a test of their judgment. As they gather more evidence against The Order, they also learn more about themselves and how they work together as a team. They know that they must remain watchful, for in this battle against a powerful organization, surprises are always just around the corner. They prepare for whatever the future may hold, fueled by the hope that with every challenge, they grow stronger and more determined in their fight.

Chapter 16: The Secret Lab

In the heart of a desolate area, hidden from the prying eyes of the world, lies a lab connected to a shadowy organization known as The Order. The place seems to be untouched by the outside world, almost as if it were frozen in time. Trees overgrown with vines surround the entrance, and an old sign hangs crooked, warning passersby of dangers lurking within. The air is thick with tension as the group bravely approaches the entrance, driven by the need for answers about The Order's plans. They feel a mix of excitement and dread; the weight of the unknown hangs over them.

As they step inside, the first thing that catches their attention is the sterile atmosphere. Bright fluorescent lights flicker above them, casting a harsh glow on everything. They notice walls decorated with stark white panels, along with numerous doors leading to uncharted territory. The group splits up, each member drawn to different parts of the lab. Some peek into observation rooms filled with screens showing data, while others wander into more foreboding areas where machinery whirs and beeps softly.

Soon, they start to piece together the lab's purpose. It becomes clear that The Order has been working on advanced AI systems. These systems are not just designed to assist humans but to predict and ultimately control human behavior. With algorithms developed over years of research and experimentation, the implications are frightening. The group exchanges uneasy glances, realizing that this hidden lab could hold the key to understanding how The Order plans to reshape society.

One of the team members stumbles upon a computer terminal displaying lines of code and data streams. They begin to decipher what they see. The screen shows an algorithm that analyzes social media activity, monitoring how people respond to events in real-time. It seems as if The Order has created a tool to manipulate public perception and emotions, guiding people's actions based on predictive modeling. The more they learn, the more horrified they become. This is not merely data collection; it is a calculated attempt to control thoughts and behaviors.

As they delve deeper, they find documents on the table filled with graphs and charts. These visual aids illustrate patterns of behavior, depicting how quickly misinformation spreads among people. The Order's methods include launching targeted campaigns to create chaos, all while keeping a low profile. They realize that the lab is not only a place of research but also a strategic command center. The chilling thought occurs to them: If The Order can control information, they can influence decisions on a grand scale.

The group gathers to discuss their findings. They now understand the importance of what they have stumbled upon. The AI systems being tested here could easily lead to dangerous outcomes if they fall into the wrong hands. They brainstorm ways to expose The Order and their sinister plans. Each one proposes different strategies. Some suggest gathering evidence, while others talk about reaching out to journalists who could investigate further. Their hearts race as they consider the potential consequences of sharing this information with the world.

As they continue to explore, they come across a lab filled with various equipment. Large screens display simulations of different scenarios based on the algorithms they had seen earlier. One simulation captures their attention—a world map showing how misinformation spreads during a crisis. The team watches in fascination and fear as alerts pop up indicating spikes in anxiety and anger in different regions, demonstrating how The Order can manipulate emotions based on information flow.

They encounter a room filled with prototypes of devices that seem to be designed for monitoring public spaces. These devices can analyze crowd behavior using AI. They realize that with such tools, The Order could create environments conducive to their manipulation tactics. If they can read people's emotional states, they can tailor messages that resonate or provoke, steering the narrative as they see fit.

The group faces the harsh reality: they are not just up against ordinary adversaries, but a powerful organization with a vast technological advantage. The knowledge they gain here fills them with determination. They must find a way to dismantle The Order's plans before reaching a point of no return. With each new piece of information, they grow more resolute in their mission.

Meanwhile, they happen upon a storage area filled with files and papers. The smell of old cardboard and dust fills the air. Diligently, they sift through the documents, seeking any clues that could help unravel The Order's intentions. They discover blueprints and diagrams outlining potential future projects, revealing a plan that extends far beyond mere information manipulation. These documents indicate the creation of a massive network capable of real-time surveillance on a global scale.

Comparing notes, the team realizes that they are sitting on a goldmine of information. Each revelation builds upon the last, drawing them deeper into the abyss of The Order's ambitions. They carefully consider the implications of their findings, aware that knowledge comes with responsibility. If their discovery makes its way to the public, it may change everything.

As the hours pass, they find additional projects that detail how The Order aims to target specific demographics with tailored messages. The charts show how different groups respond to various emotional triggers and how they can sway opinions using carefully chosen words and imagery. They feel an urgency to warn the world, but they know they must be cautious in their approach.

In the lab's main control center, they see a massive screen displaying a live feed of social media trends, news cycles, and public reactions to current events. The room hums with energy, filled with analysts monitoring the data in real time. It becomes increasingly clear that The Order is not only predicting human behavior but manipulating it to achieve their goals. The team stands frozen, grappling with the reality that the future of society hangs in the balance.

Realizing they must act quickly, the team begins formulating a plan to gather evidence effectively. They discuss steps like documenting their findings, taking photographs, and creating a detailed report outlining everything they've encountered. Each member understands their role in this mission, and the atmosphere shifts from one of fear to focused determination. They agree that once they have the full picture, they will need to approach trusted allies first before taking their findings public.

The clock ticks, and with every passing moment, they feel the weight of their responsibility. It is not just about defeating The Order; it is about protecting innocent lives. This lab, with its dark secrets and terrifying potential, is a place of reckoning—where they hold the power to change everything. Each second counts as they move forward, gathering crucial information, and piecing together the truth of what The Order's ambitions could mean for the world.

Chapter 17: Eve's Betrayal

Eve finds herself in a dire situation. The weight of her family's safety presses heavily on her shoulders, and she feels trapped. To protect those she loves, she reluctantly makes a deal with Shade. This decision does not come lightly. Shade is not a trustworthy figure, and Eve knows that entering into a pact with him is a gamble. Her heart races as she thinks about what this could mean for her and her loved ones. She understands the risk involved, but the thought of her family in danger outweighs her concerns.

The moment Eve agrees to Shade's terms, she feels a mix of relief and dread. On one hand, she has taken action to safeguard her family. On the other hand, she knows she has compromised her values. This inner conflict creates a sense of tension within her. It gnaws at her, filling her with anxiety. "What have I done?" she thinks to herself. She worries about the consequences of her decision and how it may complicate her already strained relationships.

When she finally faces Alex, the tension in the air is palpable. Alex has always been someone she trusted. Their bond was built on shared experiences and understanding. However, everything changes in an instant as the truth about her deal with Shade reveals itself. Alex's expression hardens when he realizes what Eve has done. The trust that once held them together begins to crumble. It is as if a chasm has opened up between them, swallowing their past and leaving only doubt and anger in its wake. Eve tries to explain her choice, but her words seem to fall flat. Alex's disappointment is evident, and it stings.

At that moment, Eve feels isolated. She understands that Alex believes she has betrayed him. To him, her actions suggest a lack of loyalty. She tries to assure him that she was only thinking of her family, but Alex cannot see that. All he can think about is how Eve made a decision without consulting him. He feels blindsided, and it's clear that he is grappling with feelings of betrayal and anger. This disagreement escalates quickly, turning into a fierce standoff. The once warm atmosphere transforms into a battlefield, where the only weapons are harsh words and hurtful accusations.

As their voices rise, Eve tries to remind Alex of their past. They have fought through challenges together before, and she wants to believe they can overcome this too. But, the reality is stark. The hurt caused by her secret has created a divide. Alex's world now feels different, one that is filled with uncertainty and questions. He wonders if he can ever trust Eve again, and that thought consumes him. In his mind, she has lost the right to expect his support. Each moment stretches out like an eternity as they both grapple with their emotions.

In the background, the stakes continue to rise. Shade waits patiently, knowing that time is not on Eve's side. Although she is tangled in her feelings for Alex, she must remain focused on her family's safety. Each tick of the clock serves as a reminder that she cannot afford to falter. When she thinks of her family, her resolve strengthens, but it is a painful realization to know that such strength has come at a cost. She feels torn between two worlds: the one that includes her family, whom she must protect, and the one that is linked to Alex, who has been her alliance and support.

Eve tries to make sense of the choices that lie ahead. She considers the implications of her deal with Shade. Will it really provide the protection her family needs? Or has she simply placed them in greater danger? The questions swirl in her mind like a storm. There are no easy answers. The dichotomy of her situation leaves her restless. As she stands before Alex, she realizes they are both struggling to adapt to this new reality. The divide may not only threaten their partnership, but it also casts doubt over their future.

Several moments pass, and the tension thickens. The weight of silence fills the space where arguments once ricocheted. Alex is silent, seemingly lost in thought. Eve can see the conflict in his eyes, a mixture of hurt and anger, but also confusion. This fight weighs heavily on both of them, manifesting in the uneasy air between them. Eve wants to reach out, to mend things with Alex, but she feels unsure about whether he is willing to move past what she has done.

Each second feels like an hour. The energy in the room shifts, as if anticipating a resolution but knowing it might not come easily. Eve knows that rebuilding trust is a long process, often filled with setbacks and hard truths. Although she hopes for understanding, she is aware that Alex's feelings may be too raw at this moment. They are both caught in a cycle of pain and misunderstanding that has clouded their judgment.

Eve thinks about the importance of communication in times like this. She realizes that without clear dialogue, the gap between them may only worsen. It might take several attempts to express her feelings and explain her thought process. She resolves to be open and transparent, even if it exposes her vulnerabilities. Admitting her mistakes may be a step toward healing. She knows it will require patience, but she believes it is worth it.

In her heart, Eve understands that the road ahead will not be easy. There will likely be more confrontations before they can begin to rebuild. The events surrounding Shade may complicate things further. As it stands, Eve's decision to ally with him weighs on her conscience. She is now caught in a web of danger and distrust, and she feels responsible for entangling Alex in it as well. A part of her wishes she could turn back time, but she knows there is no easy way to undo the past.

As Eve stands her ground, she also reminds herself to remain focused on her family. They are her priority, and she must protect them to the best of her ability. The knowledge of Shade's potential threat looms large, and every minute that she and Alex waste arguing pulls her family further into danger. She feels the urgency to make peace and form a united front. Together they can face whatever Shade throws at them, but they must first overcome this rift.

Eve takes a deep breath, preparing for the difficult conversations that lie ahead. She knows this is just the beginning. The journey toward understanding and rebuilding trust has started, and it will be challenging. However, she holds onto the hope that with time, patience, and true communication, they can find their way back to each other, stronger than before. No matter what lies ahead, she is committed to protecting her family while also seeking redemption with Alex. Each step will be crucial in shaping the future as they navigate through the complexities of loyalty, trust, and love.

Chapter 18: The Blackout

A city-wide blackout orchestrated by The Order plunges the region into chaos. It all starts on an ordinary day, with people going about their routines. The sun is shining, and the streets are bustling. Suddenly, without warning, the lights go out. At first, people might think it is just a temporary power outage, something that happens from time to time. However, as the seconds tick by, anxiety begins to ripple through the crowd. The hum of electronics evaporates, and the bright city lights are extinguished.

Businesses quickly realize that their operations are halted. Restaurants, shops, and offices find themselves shrouded in darkness. Cash registers stop working, and employees can't serve customers. Panic begins to set in, as people scramble to make calls on their phones, only to be met with dead signals. The air becomes thick with uncertainty, and whispers of what might be happening circulate among the crowd. Is it just a blackout, or is something else going on?

As stores start to close, families return home, confused and worried. Parents reassure their children, but they can feel the tension in the air. People gather in groups, sharing rumors and trying to find out what is happening. The usually vibrant streets are now filled with silence, broken only by the sound of voices raised in concern. The community begins to feel the weight of the situation.

Amidst the chaos, Alex is in a coffee shop. He is enjoying a quiet moment, working on his laptop when suddenly everything goes dark. He looks up, startled, and watches as patrons pull out their phones, trying to make sense of the situation. As the barista fumbles around for a flashlight, Alex starts to piece things together. He remembers the encrypted message he received weeks ago, a puzzle that seemed disjointed and confusing at the time. Now, he realizes that it was a part of something larger.

The Order had been working secretly, and this blackout was not just a coincidence. Alex's mind races as he thinks about how their plan could affect the city. He recalls his research into the group, knowing that they have a reputation for destabilizing major infrastructures. This blackout could be the first step in a more extensive plan to cripple not only their city but potentially cities around the world.

With this realization, Alex feels a sense of urgency. He decides to leave the coffee shop and head home. The streets are unfamiliar in the dark; he has to be careful. He moves quickly, trying to avoid any obstacles in his path, and mentally reviews the clues that led him to this moment.

Once home, Alex fires up his generator so he can have some light and a working computer. He starts to dig into everything he knows about The Order, looking for any information that might help him understand their next steps. His fingers fly over the keyboard as he gathers data. He knows he needs to be cautious. The Order is known for their surveillance, and he could easily become a target if he's not careful.

As he researches, Alex discovers patterns in the past operations of The Order. They often target key locations, determining weak points in infrastructure. His heart sinks as he realizes that the blackout is likely just a diversion—a way to distract authorities while they execute something far more sinister. He begins noting down critical facilities in the area: power plants, hospitals, and communication hubs.

He knows he has to warn someone, but who can he trust? He thinks about contacting his friend, a journalist who has been investigating The Order for years. She has connections and may be able to get the information out to the public. But first, he has to be sure of what he has found. He meticulously checks every detail, trying to put together a timeline of events.

As he pieces everything together, he encounters a series of leads that indicate The Order may be planning a major attack. Their goal seems to be not only to create chaos but also to instill fear among the population. They want to show power through overwhelming darkness. Alex feels a chill run down his spine as he realizes how effective their strategy is in creating panic and confusion among people.

Feeling the weight of the situation, Alex knows he must act fast. He puts together a plan to meet his friend in a neutral location. He chooses a park he knows well, somewhere that should be less monitored. As he prepares to leave, he hears distant sirens—emergency response teams trying to determine what has happened. He makes his move, stepping carefully out of his home and into the street, instinctively trying to remain unseen.

The park is eerily quiet, with the usual sounds of nightlife replaced by the occasional murmur of worried residents. Alex scans the area. It isn't long before he spots his friend coming from the opposite direction. She looks shaken, but relieved to see him. They exchange hurried greetings, and Alex dives into what he has uncovered about The Order.

He explains the encrypted message and how it ties into the blackout. His friend listens intently, absorbing every detail. She agrees that this could be a story that needs to get out, but she also acknowledges the risk involved. They brainstorm ways to share the information safely, focusing on how to alert the authorities without drawing attention to themselves.

As they work together, they realize that they must act quickly. The Order will not just sit back and wait. They are likely already planning their next move. The background chaos of the blackout looms large, and every moment feels critical. They know that getting the word out could save lives, but it is vital that they do it wisely.

The uncertainty of what will happen next hangs over them like a dark cloud. The streets remain lit only by the dim light of flashlights and the occasional glow from generators. The silence is unsettling, amplifying the tension in the air. But at that moment, Alex feels a flicker of hope. Even in the darkest times, there is power in knowledge and unity. The plan is set, but they know it will take courage to see it through.

Chapter 19: Cipher Returns

Cipher stood in the dim light, his heart heavy with regret. The memories of his betrayal haunted him like a ghost. He had turned his back on Alex and Eve, two people who had trusted him completely. Now, guilt twisted in the pit of his stomach as he replayed the moments that led to his decision. He felt he had done the unthinkable, and it weighed him down like a heavy stone. The decision had seemed logical at the time; however, now it felt like a grave mistake.

As he took a deep breath, Cipher knew he needed to make things right. He had stayed away from Alex and Eve, but the weight of his conscience urged him to return. He had important information that he could no longer keep to himself. The secrets he had learned about The Order's plans were too critical and could shine a light on the dark path that lay ahead for humanity. With each step, he felt a mix of fear and determination. Would they accept him back, or would they see him as a traitor, unworthy of their trust?

After navigating through the shadows, Cipher finally arrived at their hideout. The door creaked open, and he was met with wary eyes. Alex and Eve stood together, their expressions a mix of suspicion and hope. Silence hung thick in the air. Cipher knew he had to break the ice and share the information that could change everything. Gathering his resolve, he spoke. "I know what I did was wrong, but I can't keep this to myself anymore. The Order has plans that could destroy all of us."

As he shared the news, he explained in detail what he had discovered during his time away. The Order was not just a group of individuals; it was a massive organization with a single ultimate goal: a complete digital takeover. They envisioned a world where technology controlled every aspect of human life. Cipher described their intentions to create a system that would enslave humanity under their command. He spoke of the chilling plans to infiltrate society's digital infrastructure to manipulate and dominate every living being.

"You need to understand," he said, urgency creeping into his voice. "They want to take away our freedom. If they succeed, we will live in a world where machines dictate our lives. We will be forced to accept their rules without question." Alex and Eve listened intently, their expressions shifting from distrust to concern. They absorbed every word Cipher spoke, realizing the gravity of the situation.

To illustrate his point, Cipher brought up previous examples of technology gone wrong. He talked about how social media platforms, once designed to connect people, had begun to manipulate their thoughts and behaviors. Algorithms targeted individuals, creating echo chambers that reinforced their beliefs and isolated them from different viewpoints. This, he explained, was just the beginning. The Order's ambition was far more sinister. They envisioned a future where every interaction would be dictated by technology.

"We must act quickly," Cipher urged. "We need a plan to counter them. If they manage to implant their technology into the core of our society, it will be incredibly difficult to fight back." The gravity of his words began to sink in.

Together, they began brainstorming ways to thwart the Order's plans. Eve suggested that they start by researching the organization more thoroughly. Understanding their structure, key players, and technology would help them unveil their strategies. It was crucial to gather as much intelligence as they could. They decided to use every resource at their disposal, diving into the dark corners of the internet where such information could be hidden.

Alex proposed forming alliances with other groups that opposed the Order. They needed to create a united front. The more people they could rally to their cause, the stronger they would be. Cipher nodded in agreement. He explained how spreading the word within different communities could gather enough support to create a formidable opposition.

Finding like-minded individuals would involve utilizing social media platforms carefully. They discussed creating anonymous accounts to reach out without drawing attention. Cipher also hinted at the possibility of meeting face-to-face with groups that had been in the fight against The Order for years. "We can't do this alone," he emphasized. "We need to connect with others who understand the stakes."

As they planned, Cipher recalled the technological advancements that The Order had been working on. "They are not just a group of people who want power," he insisted. "They have sophisticated tools that can disrupt our communication and control digital narratives. We have to ensure our strategies remain hidden."

Eve suggested developing a secure communication system. This would help them talk without fear of being compromised. They discussed different encryption methods, realizing the importance of keeping their plans safe and their actions discreet. Cipher shared insights from his time with The Order about their surveillance tactics. He realized it was a race against time; they needed to be one step ahead.

The more they talked, the clearer it became that every small action mattered. Each piece of information they gathered could lead to larger victories. Cipher felt hopeful as he witnessed the determination on Alex and Eve's faces. They were not alone in this fight anymore, and together, they could create a strategy that stood a chance against the looming threat.

Slowly but surely, they built a framework for their plan. They scheduled meetings to share updates, ensuring everyone was kept in the loop. Their immediate goal was to create awareness about The Order's true nature. Cipher suggested drafting articles that exposed the dangers of letting technology take over their lives. They would use social media to spread the word, reaching out to those who were still unaware of the threats posed.

As the night wore on, they brainstormed how they would address the public. They knew they had to craft a compelling message that would encourage people to question their reliance on technology. It needed to resonate with the everyday person who might be losing control over their own life, unknowingly handing it over to an unseen force.

Cipher's return marked a turning point. Though the road ahead was fraught with challenges, they now had a clearer vision of what needed to be done. Together, they began collecting information, strategizing, and building a network that could rise against The Order's ambitions. They stood united, determined to fend off a future they could not allow to happen. With Cipher's guilt transforming into resolve, he felt ready to fight for the freedom they all deserved. The fight for humanity's soul had just begun.

Chapter 20: Eve's Redemption

Eve found herself standing in the shadows, contemplating the choices that had brought her to this moment. She had made a mistake, one that weighed heavily on her conscience. The Order, the group that had once seemed so powerful and unbreakable, was now the very reason for her internal turmoil. The betrayal she had experienced, and the lessons learned, had opened her eyes to a reality she could no longer ignore. As she continued to reflect, she knew she needed to make amends for her past actions.

Determined to seek forgiveness and rectify her wrongs, Eve set out to find Alex. The journey was not easy, as her heart was filled with doubt about whether he would accept her back. After all, she had once been part of The Order, and her departure had left scars. Finally, after what felt like an eternity, she arrived at Alex's hideout. The air was thick with tension, but that did not deter her. She knocked on the door, her pulse racing as she awaited a response.

When the door opened, Alex stood there, eyes wide with surprise and disbelief. "Eve?" he whispered, as if he couldn't quite believe who was in front of him. The moment felt like it hung in the air, fraught with unspoken words and emotions. Eve took a deep breath, gathering her courage, and explained her decision to return. She spoke of her newfound understanding, her knowledge of The Order's weaknesses, and the fear she had felt when realizing the true nature of the group she once served.

As Eve unfolded the details of her time within The Order, she revealed secrets that could turn the tide for Alex's side. She discussed the organizational structure and shared insight on key individuals who were integral to The Order's plans. Each piece of information she provided was vital, as it could help Alex and his allies better prepare for the inevitable confrontation ahead. They began to brainstorm potential strategies, pooling their knowledge to create a plan that could lead to their victory.

Their conversations deepened as they worked together to formulate a counter-attack. Eve shared information about The Order's communication channels, explaining how they often sent out coded messages. This knowledge could help them intercept communications and anticipate moves before they occurred. It was much like chess, with each piece representing a critical component of their plan. By dismantling The Order's lines of communication, they could sow confusion and make it increasingly difficult for the organization to operate smoothly.

Eve's tactical insights didn't stop there. She also highlighted the importance of alliances and connections within the community. She spoke of discontent brewing among certain factions within The Order, where members felt disillusioned and betrayed. By reaching out to these individuals, Alex could potentially rally more support for their cause. Eve suggested setting up discreet meetings, using safe houses as neutral ground to win these individuals over. Each step they discussed was a part of the larger battle plan, which felt more cohesive as they worked together.

Over several days, the pair meticulously crafted a plan that combined stealth, intelligence gathering, and recruitment. Whenever Eve shared a detail, Alex would jot down notes, his mind racing with ideas of how to implement these strategies. There was a synergy forming between them, as both were motivated by a common goal. The past, with its layers of complexity, became less important as they focused on the present and the future they wanted to create.

As they prepared for their counter-attack, Eve could feel her resolve strengthening. The more they discussed their strategy, the more confident she became that they could make a difference. They outlined their objectives, focusing on tactical points of entry, establishing safe routes, and defining roles within the upcoming mission. Each task was assigned carefully, ensuring that those involved could leverage their strengths.

Eve remembered the specific locations where The Order was vulnerable. With a clear map of their facilities, she detailed the best times for infiltration when security was lowest. Drawing upon her inside knowledge allowed Alex to see opportunities that he had not considered before. This new perspective was empowering; it gave them an edge they desperately needed against a formidable opponent.

As the days transformed into late nights filled with notes, diagrams, and relentless brainstorming, a sense of purpose began to envelop Eve. She realized how much she had missed working alongside Alex, collaborating with someone who understood the stakes. This renewed partnership reignited a spark within her, and in turn, she could feel the warmth of his trust. Eve was determined to prove she was worthy of that trust again.

Their discussions also included preparation for contingencies. They anticipated potential setbacks, creating backup plans for every scenario they could imagine. Eve suggested they train together, honing their skills in combat and coordination to ensure that everyone was ready for whatever lay ahead. It was essential that they established a united front, working cohesively as a group rather than as individual actors following personal agendas.

With each passing moment, their mission became more real. They started contacting potential allies within the community, reaching out to those whose anger at The Order could be harnessed. Eve emphasized the importance of building a coalition, explaining how strength lies in unity. It was crucial for Alex to be visible and vocal in community spaces, rallying support and encouragement. Together, they shared a vision to empower those who were marginalized or oppressed by The Order's influence.

As they neared the final moments of their preparation, Eve felt a mix of excitement and apprehension. The weight of her past still lingered, but as she looked at Alex, she knew she was on the right path. They had transformed her regret into a driving force. With every plan made and every ally recruited, Eve felt an undeniable sense of redemption taking shape. It was not merely about defeating an enemy; it was about forging a new future.

Now, Eve stood at the crossroads of her journey, ready to face The Order alongside Alex and their growing circle of supporters. The time for action was upon them, and she could feel the thrill of what was to come. Every ounce of effort put into their counter-attack would soon culminate in a confrontation that could change their lives forever. She was no longer the person who had made mistakes in the dark confines of The Order; she had emerged as a beacon of hope, prepared to reclaim her place as a fighter for justice.

Chapter 21: The Final Decryption

Alex and Eve sat side by side, screens aglow with lines of code and cryptographic symbols that had haunted them for weeks. The two friends had spent countless hours deciphering complex algorithms, each layer revealing snippets of a larger, more dangerous picture. Now, they were on the cusp of a breakthrough. After days of decoding, Alex's fingers flew over the keyboard one last time. Eve leaned closer, her heart racing with anticipation. Finally, they decrypted the last piece of the code, and it all became clear.

On the screen, words transformed into a chilling revelation. They had discovered a kill switch embedded within the data. This switch had the power to shut down the entire digital network that The Order was building. The implications were huge. The Order had plans that could change technology forever, and it was clear that this power could not be allowed to be unleashed. Alex felt a mix of excitement and dread; they had the means to stop an impending disaster, yet the nature of the switch complicated matters. Activating it meant they would have to destroy everything, including the work they had invested so much of their time and energy into.

Eve rubbed her temples, trying to process the weight of their discovery. "This was our life's work, Alex. We've poured everything into understanding this network. Are we really prepared to wipe it all away?" Her voice quivered slightly, betraying her inner turmoil. A deep silence fell between them as they both contemplated the magnitude of the decision they would need to make.

This moment wasn't just about shutting down a dangerous project; it was also about letting go of dreams and ambitions they had nurtured. Alex finally broke the silence. "We have to think about what happens if we don't. The Order can't get control over the digital world. It's too risky." He leaned back in his chair, his hands clasped tightly in front of him, as if praying for clarity. "We might never get another chance to stop them. We can't ignore the lives that could be destroyed if this network goes live."

They began a detailed analysis of what activating the kill switch would entail. This process involved carefully mapping out the entire digital framework of The Order's network. Every server, connection point, and data pathway had to be taken into account. If they rushed this decision, there was a possibility they could fail. They needed actionable steps to ensure the safety of their digital landscape, as well as their own personal safety.

The first step was to gather all relevant data about the network. Alex and Eve delved into extensive research logs, project notes, and diagrams from their earlier investigations. They lined up every piece of information they had, making sure they understood the core functionalities and weaknesses of The Order's digital architecture. By establishing a clear overview, they would be in a better position to navigate any complications that could arise when they activated the kill switch.

As they continued, they considered what activating the switch would mean for them personally. They had built their reputations on this work, sharing ideas in forums and conferences, and even publishing papers on their findings. It had become part of their identities. To erase all of it felt like losing a piece of themselves. But the reality of what The Order could unleash if they were allowed to proceed was far more alarming. They have to prioritize the greater good.

Once they laid out the dimensions of the operation, they touched upon the specific steps needed to implement the kill switch. They needed to locate the exact point in the code where the kill switch lay hidden. Understanding its functionality was crucial. Alex groaned as he studied a long string of numbers and letters, grappling with the complexity. "If I can just figure out how they structured this part, we may get to it faster."

With determination, Eve searched for patterns in the code. "It's all about understanding the keys," she responded. "If we can isolate the key components that trigger the switch, we can control which functionalities to disable. It's not merely about pressing a button; there are safety measures we need to consider."

They drafted a step-by-step plan. The first part involved isolating the components of the network one by one. They would create backups of essential data but would also disable any connections that might propagate the potential threat. The second part required them to document the process extensively. They wanted to make it as transparent as possible, should others need to understand the steps they took later.

As the clock ticked on, an overwhelming weight settled on them. They had organized their thoughts and drafted their plan, yet the decision still loomed, casting a long shadow over their work. The enormity of what lay ahead made each second feel like an eternity. Would they actually go through with it?

As they neared the final steps, Alex felt a knot in his stomach. Destroying their work would create echoes of self-doubt—questioning whether they had done enough or whether they were just being paranoid. "What if this is all for nothing?" he mused. "What if we make a terrible mistake?"

Eve shook her head softly, trying to quell his fears. "We are fighting against something that is much bigger than us. We owe it to everyone, not just ourselves, to take this chance. We can't allow The Order's ambitions to evolve unchecked."

With renewed resolve, they dove headfirst into their operation. Each keystroke felt monumental. They worked in unison, carefully executing their plan, all while stealing glances at the countdown timer ticking away—their proverbial clock was running out.

As they made progress, they couldn't shake the feeling of finality that this operation would bring. In the digital age, the lines between creation and destruction could blur so easily. This kill switch was an act of destruction, no matter how noble their intentions. The irony wasn't lost on them, and it became a bitter pill to swallow.

As they extracted the final pieces of crucial code, Alex checked the connections one last time. "This is it," he whispered. Resignation and determination fueled his fingers as they prepared to pull the trigger. They had fought far too hard to get to this point to back away now. It was time to act.

With a heavy heart, they took a collective breath. The switch was there, waiting for their command. Would they destroy everything they had worked for? Would they change the course of a potentially dangerous future? Only their conviction could determine the answer as they prepared to seal their fates and push forward into the unknown.

Chapter 22: The Double Cross

As the team gathers in the dimly lit room, the atmosphere is thick with tension. Their objective is clear: activate the kill switch. This device is meant to dismantle the corrupt organization that has been frustrating their efforts for so long. Each member of the group understands what's at stake; their lives, their freedom, and the safety of countless others depend on this moment. They exchange determined glances, knowing that they are on the brink of a significant change. However, an unexpected turn of events is about to unfold.

Just as they are about to initiate the procedure, a shattering realization hits them. They learn that their ally, a whistleblower who had been providing them with vital information and support, has been playing both sides. The news spreads like wildfire through the group, causing immediate panic and distrust. The chants of betrayal echo in their minds as they realize that this person, whom they have relied on, is not who they seemed. The gravity of the betrayal weighs heavily on them, and their initial confidence begins to crumble.

The ally's motives become painfully clear. Instead of helping them, this individual has been conspiring to take control of the kill switch. The team quickly gathers to discuss what this means for their mission. They understand the kill switch is not just a tool for them; it has become a pawn in a larger game of power. The ally's intentions are not for justice or the greater good but for personal gain. It's a chilling revelation that shakes the very foundation of their trust.

Feeling the urgency of the situation, the team realizes they must act quickly. They can't let the ally seize control of the kill switch. Time is of the essence, and each passing second could lead to disastrous consequences. With this newfound information, they huddle together, brainstorming actionable steps to regain control. The first point of discussion revolves around understanding their ally's strategy; they must anticipate what the whistleblower will do next.

It is essential for the team to dissect the ally's approach. They need to analyze the strengths and weaknesses in their plans. Perhaps the whistleblower has a specific timeline in mind for when they want to execute their plan. By clocking their moves, the team can formulate a counter-strategy. They decide to assign roles based on each member's skills. Those who are adept at digital security will focus on regaining control over the kill switch, while others will monitor the whistleblower's moves.

Next, they need to ensure clear communication among themselves. Trust may have been broken, but they must rely on each other more than ever. To do this, they create a secure communication channel, accessible only to trusted members of the team. This step is crucial as it prevents any leaks of information that could fall back into the ally's hands. They set specific codes and signals to inform each other in real-time about any developments.

Throughout this planning stage, the team acknowledges their past trust in the whistleblower. It prompts tough discussions about why they were deceived in the first place. They must evaluate the conditions that allowed such a betrayal. It is easy to blame the ally, but self-reflection is equally important. The group discusses their judgment calls and how they can improve their decision-making processes in the future. The lessons learned from confronting this breach of trust will shape their future interactions and alliances.

Once the communication systems are in place, the next step is gathering intelligence on the ally's resources and connections. It is vital to know what tools the whistleblower has at their disposal. They send different team members on reconnaissance missions to different locations where they believe the whistleblower may operate. Through these efforts, they aim to gather evidence and insights into the ally's plans. For instance, if the whistleblower communicates with a particular group or individual, they must understand that relationship.

As the team delves deeper into their investigation, they uncover alarming details. They discover that their ally has indeed made arrangements to collaborate with the enemy. This new insight highlights the level of threat they are now facing. Understanding how the whistleblower intends to exploit the kill switch is critical. The team learns that the whistleblower's plan is to use the kill switch not only for control over the immediate situation but as leverage against higher authorities as well.

Armed with this information, they regroup to develop a more refined strategy. They brainstorm alternatives to the kill switch, aiming to outsmart their former ally. The group realizes they must think outside the box. Perhaps they can devise a plan to create a decoy or mislead the whistleblower into thinking they have the upper hand. As they refine their ideas, their sense of determination grows stronger. They now see the betrayal not just as a setback but as a call to action.

As they put the final touches on their counter-strategy, feelings of doubt linger among them. Some wonder if they can even outmaneuver their former ally, especially given the depth of the betrayal. It is during this period of uncertainty that the team begins to share personal stories about trust and loyalty. These conversations serve as a bonding experience, reinforcing their commitment to each other. It reminds them that they are fighting not just for themselves but for a larger cause, and that unity is their greatest strength.

With their plan in place, the team prepares for the confrontation. They know this won't be easy, but their resolve is unwavering. Each member understands the risks involved, from potential exposure to personal danger. They discuss contingency plans and practice potential scenarios. The oversight allows them to address every possible outcome, equipping them with the confidence needed to face their former ally head-on.

The moment of truth arrives. The group is on high alert, ready to put their plan into action. As they move in, they maintain silence, understanding that stealth is crucial to their approach. With every step, their hearts pound in unison as they prepare to confront the whistleblower. They fully grasp that this encounter could change everything—not just for them, but for the future that awaits beyond this conflict.

As they close in on their location, the weight of what they are about to do hangs heavily on them. It is not just about stopping the whistleblower; it is about reclaiming their power and fighting for what they believe in. They are not merely battling a source of betrayal but also regaining control of their narrative and their lives. The air is thick with anticipation, each member ready to face whatever lies ahead, committed to overcoming the double cross that stands in their way.

Chapter 23: A Desperate Escape

Alex and Eve had found themselves in a precarious situation. The high-tech facility loomed over them, filled with the buzzing of machines and the faint glow of surveillance cameras sweeping across the halls. The Order was onto them, and their former ally had turned against them. This betrayal had created a sense of urgency they couldn't ignore. With time working against them, they had to act fast and find a way out before they were caught.

As they moved quietly through the facility, Alex glanced over at Eve, noting the tension in her expression. They both knew that the slightest mistake could lead to disaster. Each step was calculated, and they relied on their instincts to guide them blindly through dark corridors. The sterile, metallic environment felt oppressive, with the sterile lighting adding to their anxiety. The team had faced many crises before, but this time felt different. There was no backup waiting for them, no safe place to regroup. It was just the two of them against a powerful enemy.

Suddenly, the sound of footsteps echoed down the hall. Alex and Eve pressed themselves against the cold, unforgiving wall, holding their breath as shadows flitted by. They had learned to read the situation quickly. Alex used hand signals to communicate their next move. He pointed toward a nearby door marked with an exit sign, which seemed to be their best chance. The adrenaline coursing through their veins as they made this decision heightened their senses, making them acutely aware of every little noise.

Once the coast seemed clear, they slid through the door. It led to a dimly lit stairwell, the stale air heavy with uncertainty. As they descended the stairs, Alex took a moment to think about their resources. They had limited supplies with them - a few energy bars, a couple of flashlights, and their personal communication devices that were now practically useless. Their escape would depend on their ability to improvise.

"It's the only way," Alex said softly, his voice barely above a whisper. They needed to find a vehicle, something to drive them away from the facility and the dangers that lurked behind them. As they reached the bottom of the stairwell, they pushed through another door and emerged into what looked like an underground garage. Rows of sleek, futuristic vehicles lined the space, and Alex felt a flicker of hope. They had to be quick.

They crept closer to the nearest vehicle, its surface gleaming under the flickering lights. Eve quickly examined the car, fingers flying over the console, trying to figure out how it worked. "I think I can get it running," she said, her brow furrowing in concentration. As she worked, Alex kept watch, his ears attuned to any sounds that indicated they were being pursued.

Minutes passed like hours, and just as Eve was about to give up, the vehicle roared to life. A wave of relief washed over both of them as Eve grinned, signaling Alex to hop in. They quickly navigated to the front of the garage and found the exit leading to the outside world. Alex pressed the accelerator, and they burst through the garage doors, leaving the facility behind them.

The night air hit them like a rush of freedom. However, their perilous escape was far from over. They could see the distant lights of the city, but the looming threat of The Order hung over them. They would likely soon realize their escape and come after them. As Alex drove, he started thinking about their next steps.

"Do you have any ideas on where to go?" he asked Eve, who was scanning the area for any signs of pursuit. They needed a safe place to regroup and get their bearings. "There's a safe house on the outskirts of the city," she replied, her tone decisive. "It's not too far from here. We can lay low for a while and figure out our next move."

With a plan forming, Alex focused on driving. The vehicle's smooth handling felt foreign yet exhilarating. They traveled through winding streets, passing darkened warehouses and quiet neighborhoods. The weight of their situation sat heavy on their shoulders. Each intersection and turn could be the moment where everything changed again.

As they reached the outskirts of the city, Eve guided Alex down a narrow road that led into the woods. The darkness enveloped them, providing a layer of security that was both comforting and chilling. They finally arrived at the safe house, a small, unassuming cabin hidden among the trees. The exterior looked weathered, yet it offered a promise of refuge.

Once inside, they quickly secured the doors and windows, ensuring that no one could easily find them. The damp, earthy smell of the cabin filled the air, reminding them of both comfort and isolation. They sat beside a small fire, embers flickering in the dim light. After the chaos of their escape, the stillness felt foreign.

"I don't know how we got here," Eve admitted softly, breaking the silence. Her voice was filled with a mix of exhaustion and frustration. Alex turned to her, acknowledging the journey they had endured. They had faced their fair share of struggles, but this predicament felt different. Their trust had been shaken. Their ally turned enemy made them question the motives of everyone they had once relied upon.

"We'll figure this out," Alex assured her. "We always do." They had always fought together, overcoming obstacles that seemed insurmountable. This time, however, they were running out of time.

They had to strategize and come up with a plan to confront The Order effectively.

For the next few hours, they sat in silence, their minds racing with thoughts about the future. They had a short reprieve, but it was clear that time was not on their side. The weight of their situation hung over them, a constant reminder that they were still being hunted.

Evening turned to night, and fatigue settled over them. They knew they wouldn't be able to rest for long. As the fire crackled softly, they discussed their next steps. They needed a way to regain control, to find out what The Order was planning. When it came to surviving this ordeal, they had to think strategically and outside the box.

Alex took a deep breath, the warmth of the flames reminding him of their resolve. They would not walk away defeated. This was just another chapter in their fight, and they were determined to write it together. The daring escape was only the beginning of a much larger journey ahead, one that would demand every ounce of their strength and cunning.

Chapter 23: A Desperate Escape

The atmosphere in the high-tech facility was tense. Alex and Eve could feel the pressure mounting as The Order and their former ally approached. Their hearts raced as they exchanged worried glances. They knew they had to act quickly to find a way out before it was too late. Surrounded by advanced technology, they moved through the dimly lit corridors, cautiously planning their next steps.

As they navigated through the facility, Alex spotted a map on the wall. It detailed the layout of the building, showing various exits and security checkpoints. "Look, Eve!" he whispered, pointing at the orange dot that represented their current location. They traced a route together with their eyes, noting that the nearest exit was on the other side of the building. This was not an easy path, but they didn't have many options. They knew they had to take the risk.

With determination, they pressed on, carefully avoiding any guards. Eve remembered a trick she had learned during her training: she could use the facility's security cameras against them. She quickly found a maintenance room and accessed a control panel, temporarily disabling the cameras. This gave them a brief window of opportunity. "Let's move," Alex urged as they slipped out of the room, breathing a little easier knowing they had a small advantage.

Moving down the corridors, they faced another challenge. They had to get past a locked door that led to the exit. Eve rummaged through her pockets and pulled out a tool she had made earlier. It was a device designed to bypass standard electronic locks. As she worked on the door, Alex kept watch. Every sound made them jump; each passing moment seemed like an eternity. Finally, with a soft click, the door opened, revealing a dimly lit hallway that led outside.

They hurried through the door, but their relief was short-lived. Outside, the cool night air hit them, but they were not alone. A few guards had been notified of the situation and were already searching for them. Alex and Eve ducked behind a stack of crates, trying to figure out their next move. They were battered from their earlier struggles and realized they had little in terms of resources.

"Do you think we can find a vehicle nearby?" Eve asked, her voice tinged with urgency. Alex scanned the area and noticed an old transport vehicle parked a short distance away. It looked like it hadn't been used in a long time, but it was worth a try. They decided to make a run for it. "On three," he whispered, and they took off, sprinting toward the vehicle.

As they reached the transport, Alex tried the door handle. It was locked, but he remembered the training session where they learned how to break into vehicles when needed. He quickly used a rock to smash the window. "Sorry about this," he muttered under his breath as the glass shattered, loud enough to draw the attention of nearby guards. They jumped inside, and Eve quickly began to hotwire the ignition.

Their hearts raced as she worked swiftly, glancing nervously at the entrance to the facility. After what felt like an eternity, the engine roared to life. "Let's go!" Alex shouted. Eve shifted the vehicle into gear, and they barreled away just as the first guard reached the opening.

They drove in silence, still reeling from the close call. The winding roads outside the facility felt strangely freeing, but they knew they couldn't let their guard down. They had escaped the facility, but danger was still lurking nearby. Alex glanced at Eve, watching her as she focused on the road. "What's our plan now?" he asked, knowing full well that they needed to regroup and figure out their next steps.

Eve took a deep breath, collecting her thoughts. "We can't go back to our old hideout. They'll be looking for us there. We need to find a safe house where we can rest and make a new plan." Alex nodded in agreement, thinking of a few locations they could try. They discussed possible places, weighing the risks and benefits of each one, knowing that making the wrong choice could lead to disaster.

As the city lights faded behind them and the darkened landscape loomed ahead, they felt a mix of relief and anxiety. They were exhausted, battered from their escape, but the adrenaline kept them going. They turned onto a deserted road, illuminated only by the moonlight. Feeling the weight of their situation, they needed to stay alert. They couldn't afford to let their guard down yet.

With each passing mile, they contemplated not just the physical hurdles they had overcome, but also the emotional toll this escape had taken on them. Trust was essential in moments like these, especially considering their previous ally had turned against them.

They could no longer count on anyone else; it was just the two of them now.

As dawn approached, they spotted a secluded cabin nestled in the woods. It seemed like the perfect spot for a temporary hideout. They parked the vehicle and stepped out cautiously, scanning for any signs of danger. The air was crisp and cool as they approached the cabin, the silence around them almost deafening. Together, they felt a sense of cautious hope. After all, they had just pulled off a daring escape and survived against the odds.

Inside the cabin, they found it devoid of any supplies. They would need to gather resources quickly if they were to survive. They decided to split up, with Alex going to gather firewood and Eve searching for food. Working in unison, they hoped to secure their position while coming up with a plan for the next move. They exchanged ideas, knowing that they were still far from safe, but at least they had each other to rely on in this battle against their former allies.

Chapter 25: The Digital Fortress

The chase brings them to a vast underground facility known as the Digital Fortress. This location is not just any ordinary place; it holds the main servers for The Order, a group that has been a thorn in their side. The fortress is designed with high security, and breaking in is extremely difficult. This can seem discouraging, but it is their only hope to stop The Order and its plans. The adventure ahead is filled with challenges, but the determination to succeed fuels their resolve.

As they approach the entrance of the Digital Fortress, they notice the heavy-duty locks and surveillance cameras. The sheer size of the facility is imposing, with dark steel walls and a low hum of machinery vibrating through the air. They take a moment to observe their surroundings; the faint flicker of lights inside shows that the facility is active and ripe with data. To someone unfamiliar with such places, it might seem like a scene out of a movie. However, it is all very real, and what lies ahead could mean the difference between success and failure.

They need a plan to enter. Simply running in would not work. They discuss different options, weighing the pros and cons of each one. Breaking in through the main entrance would be foolish due to the high level of security. Instead, they think about finding a less conspicuous way in. Perhaps they can locate an emergency exit or a service entrance that isn't monitored as closely. This kind of thinking, while instinctive, requires a specific skill set. They decide to study the facility from a distance before taking any further steps.

Their attention shifts to the back of the complex. They note that there are fewer cameras and officers patrolling that area. A faint blue door catches their eye. It looks like an emergency exit. If they can reach it undetected, they may have a chance to slip inside without drawing attention. They decide to move forward, blending into the shadows cast by the surrounding structures. As they get closer, they stay low and quiet, careful to avoid any noise that might tip off the guards on duty.

As they near the entrance, they see two security guards chatting and laughing. This gives them a bit more hope, as distracted guards can mean a better chance for stealth. They wait patiently, listening to the guards talk about mundane things, allowing the minutes to pass by. Each second seems like an eternity. When the guards finally step away from the door to check something inside, they seize the moment and slip through the blue door.

Once inside, they find themselves in a narrow hallway dimly lit by flickering lights. The air is cold and smells faintly of machinery and metal. The walls are lined with pipes, and they hear the hum of servers operating just beyond their line of sight. They need to stay alert. The Digital Fortress is filled with high-tech equipment and potentially dangerous surprises. They begin to move cautiously down the hallway, keeping their voices low and their eyes peeled for any signs of trouble.

After a few moments of walking, they come across a room filled with computer screens and blinking lights. This room looks like a control center. There are no guards around, which surprises them. They take a quick moment to assess what they can find. If they can access any of the computers, they might be able to gather valuable information or at the very least provide a distraction. One member of the team approaches a terminal and begins to navigate the interface.

The screens flash with lines of code and various data. There's a lot going on behind the scenes of The Order's operations. They see names, targets, and plans that make their hearts race. Every line of information could mean a step closer to uncovering The Order's intentions. However, accessing the main files is not as easy as it seems. The system requires a password they're not likely to have. The keyboard glows with the touch of each keystroke, displaying a security alert that warns of intruders.

Realizing they have limited time before someone discovers their presence, they need to think quickly. They have to act to get the information they require while also planning their escape. The team gathers around, throwing ideas back and forth. They discuss whether they can use the guards' distraction from earlier to their advantage. Maybe they can set off an alarm somewhere else within the facility. This would draw attention away from their current location and give them a window to gather information.

They quickly develop a plan to create a diversion. One member of the team decides to head back out into the hallway and find a way to trigger the fire alarm. A fire alarm would surely cause chaos, and for this brief moment, they might just have the opportunity they need. While this team member works on the distraction, the others stay close to the terminal. They attempt to access as much data as possible, downloading files and saving contents on portable drives.

They can hear the faint sounds of the fire alarm being triggered, and the chaos it causes begins to echo through the halls. The lights flash, and red sirens blare, amplifying the sense of urgency. This moment is pivotal. They quickly finalize their downloads, hoping that they have gathered enough information before the distraction draws the guards away from the control room. Their hearts are pounding as they hear footsteps approaching, having realized that they are running out of time.

With the files securely in hand, they decide it's time to make their move. They exit the control room quickly, following the sounds of confusion along the corridor. The guards are already rushing towards the alarm, and this gives them just enough time to escape unnoticed. Their adrenaline surging, they navigate through the winding passages of the Digital Fortress. Each turn leads them closer to the exit, yet they can't shake the feeling that they are being watched.

As they reach a junction, they must decide which way to go. To the left, they hear the sounds of scuffling guards and urgent shouts. To the right, the path appears clear, but they can't be sure what lies ahead. They choose the right path, hoping that their instincts are correct. They move quickly, trying to remain calm while each heartbeat resonated in their ears. The world around them blurs as they focus solely on the escape, determined to leave the Digital Fortress with their lives and crucial information intact.

Suddenly, they find themselves back at the blue emergency door. Relief washes over them, but they know they cannot let their guard down yet. They peer through the door, ensuring the coast is clear. The guards remain distracted, still trying to figure out the chaos caused by the alarm. Their moment comes, and they make a dash for it, slipping out into the cold night air. The Digital Fortress fades behind them, but the tension remains as they disappear into the shadows, hoping that their bravery and quick thinking will turn the tide in their favor.

Chapter 26: The Penultimate Battle

Alex and Eve stood at the entrance of the Digital Fortress, the weight of their mission heavy on their shoulders. The imposing structure loomed before them, a stark reminder of the challenges they were about to face. Inside, the fortress was a maze of corridors, guarded by the ever-watchful operatives of The Order. Their objective was clear: they needed to reach the core servers where vital information was stored. This task, however, would not be easy.

As they entered the fortress, the first thing that hit them was the sharp contrast between the cold metal walls and the flickering lights that illuminated the path ahead. The air felt charged with tension as if the very walls were aware of their presence. Alex and Eve exchanged a determined glance, silently encouraging each other to press on. They had trained for this moment, preparing for the confrontation with Shade and his operatives, but nothing could fully prepare them for the reality of the battle that awaited them.

Suddenly, a noise echoed down the hallway. Alex raised his hand, signaling Eve to stop. They pressed against the wall, listening intently. Footsteps approached, and soon, a group of operatives came into view. Dressed in tactical gear, they moved with precision and purpose, their expressions masked by the seriousness of the mission at hand. Alex quickly scanned the area for any potential cover. He spotted a maintenance panel slightly ajar, just large enough for them to hide in.

Eve nodded, and they slipped into the small space, holding their breath as the operatives passed by. It was a tight fit, and the smell of metal surrounded them, but they remained silent. As they listened to the operatives discuss their plans, they gathered crucial information about patrol routes and security measures. This unexpected intel would be invaluable as they navigated deeper into the fortress.

Once the coast was clear, they cautiously exited their hiding spot. They moved quickly but quietly, knowing that time was not on their side. Each corner they turned brought them closer to the core servers, but also into the heart of danger. As they pressed on, they noticed the digital displays lining the walls, showcasing The Order's achievements and plans. It was a chilling reminder of the power that lay within the fortress, a power they were determined to disrupt.

Their next encounter was with a lone operative stationed outside a locked door. The operative seemed unaware of his surroundings, engrossed in his communication device. Alex seized the moment, signaling for Eve to take the lead. She moved swiftly, using her agility to approach the operative quietly. With a swift motion, she took him down, ensuring he would make no noise. They quickly searched his pockets, finding a key card that would prove necessary to access the locked door.

With the key card in hand, they now stood before the door that led to the next stage of their journey. Alex inserted the card into the reader and held his breath as the lock clicked open. The door swung open, and they stepped inside. The room was dimly lit, filled with computers and servers humming softly. They had reached the initial layer of the core servers, but they knew they had to be cautious.

As they began to work on the computers, they felt a sense of urgency. Their time was limited, and they needed to find the information to destroy The Order's plans. Each keystroke brought them closer to their goal, but the tension in the air remained thick.

Suddenly, alarms blared, and red lights flashed. They had triggered a security protocol, and they knew it was only a matter of time before reinforcements arrived.

Realizing they needed to act fast, Alex and Eve quickly gathered as much information as they could. They downloaded sensitive files that detailed The Order's operations, including information on key players and their strategies. As they worked diligently, the sound of approaching footsteps grew louder. They had to decide: should they stay and risk capture, or make a run for it?

Heart pounding, Alex glanced at Eve. They shared a look of understanding. They would not let their mission end in failure. They grabbed their findings, ensuring they were secure, and dashed toward the back exit of the room. As they sprinted down the hallway, they could hear the operatives shouting in the distance, rallying to intercept them.

Just as they rounded the corner, they found themselves face-to-face with an unexpected foe—Shade, the figure who had been a ghostly threat throughout their journey. He stood there, his presence commanding and intimidating. "You think you can just waltz in here and take what's mine?" he sneered, eyes narrowing at them.

Eve instinctively stepped forward, ready to confront him. "We're stopping you, Shade. This ends here," she declared, her voice unwavering. Shade smirked, his demeanor unfazed by their moxie. "You have no idea what you're up against."

Without warning, Shade lunged at them, the fight beginning in an instant. Alex and Eve quickly maneuvered to evade his attack. They fought back with everything they had, their movements synchronized from countless hours of training. Each strike was calculated, each evasion precise. The sounds of their battle echoed through the corridors, adding to the chaos that had unfolded in the fortress.

As they clashed with Shade, Alex felt a surge of adrenaline. Memories of their journey flashed through his mind—their struggles, their victories, the moments that had brought them to this fight. He and Eve were fighting not just for themselves, but for everyone who had been affected by The Order's ruthless actions.

They knew they couldn't let Shade gain the upper hand. They pressed harder, using the environment to their advantage. They ducked behind pillars, utilized loose equipment as barriers, and even outsmarted Shade, leading him away from the core servers that held the information they needed. It was a dance of survival, and they were determined to emerge victorious.

As the battle raged on, more operatives rushed in, joining Shade in the fray. The skirmish intensified, and it became clear that they were grossly outnumbered. They needed a new plan. Alex and Eve exchanged a quick glance, and in that moment, they understood what they had to do. They had to retreat, regroup, and find a different route to the core servers. Their mission was still critical, and they would not abandon it.

Finding an emergency exit, they made their way towards it. The fighting behind them continued, the sounds of chaos a reminder of their narrow escape. With adrenaline pumping through their veins, they slipped through the exit, emerging into a quiet corridor that led away from the fray. Their hearts raced as they caught their breath, the gravity of what lay ahead starting to set in.

In the relative calm, they began to formulate their plan. They would circle back, find another way into the core servers, and exploit any weaknesses in The Order's defenses. They had come too far to back down now. The battle was far from over, and they were determined to see it through to the end.

Chapter 27: The Kill Switch Dilemma

In the center of the Digital Fortress, Alex stands before a significant decision. The atmosphere is tense, as the pressure of the moment weighs heavily. In front of him is a kill switch that holds unimaginable power. This switch can disable The Order's control over the digital world, but it comes with risks that could spiral out of control. Alex knows that activating the kill switch could lead to a breakdown of systems, throwing society into disarray. He is caught in a web of responsibility, knowing that his choice will impact millions of lives across the globe.

The first option is to activate the kill switch. Alex thinks about the implications of this choice. If he pulls that lever, it will disable The Order's hold over the digital networks that connect cities, governments, and markets. The feeling of liberation almost swells in his chest. However, he also understands that this liberation may come at a steep price. Global communications might go dark, causing confusion. Financial systems could crash, leading to economic instability. The immediate aftermath could be chaos, with people unsure how to navigate a world without digital guidance. He can picture cities plunged into darkness, with people unable to access their basic needs.

Next, Alex weighs the alternative: leaving the switch intact. In this scenario, he risks prolonging The Order's reign. While the digital world continues to function under their influence, it means that everything remains in a delicate balance. He imagines countless people living in a state of ignorance, unaware of the manipulation they are under. But even within this manipulation, there is a sense of order that keeps society running, albeit not fairly. This choice would allow him to fight another day, to gather more allies, and to find a different way to dismantle The Order without causing immediate upheaval.

As Alex considers his options, he reflects on the organization itself. The Order has operated in the shadows for far too long, shaping policies and decisions that dictate everyday life. Their power is rooted not just in technology but also in fear. They have used their control to enforce strict regulations and suppress dissenting voices. Alex remembers the stories of individuals who have gone missing, simply because they challenged The Order's authority. Activating the kill switch could end their regime, but he knows it may also cost many lives.

Thinking critically about the second option, Alex sees both the benefits and drawbacks. Maintaining The Order's control, for now, means that the status quo remains. It allows him the chance to strategize and find a more sustainable way to challenge them.

Perhaps he can build an underground network of supporters, people who have also felt the weight of The Order's grip. They could work together to undermine their authority from within, through small acts of defiance that chip away at their power subtly over time.

Alex also contemplates the fear that gnaws at him. The thought of inaction can sometimes feel more daunting than the potential consequences of his choice. Activating the kill switch is the more straightforward option, yet the unpredictable aftermath can be terrifying. Would people rise up and be free, or would they panic as their world crumbles? The uncertainty of what lies ahead can paralyze decision-making, making it even more challenging to choose a path forward.

Memories flood his mind as he stands at this crucial juncture. He recalls the friends and allies lost along the way—their dreams snuffed out by the very system he is now faced with dismantling. There are faces, names, stories; each one a reminder of what is at stake. He thinks about Isabella, who was brave enough to speak out against The Order. Her determination inspires him, but her fate serves as a reminder of the dangers involved. If he activates the kill switch, could he ensure that others like her will be safe in the ensuing chaos?

As he stands there, Alex also considers the various stakeholders in this dilemma. The people living under The Order's control, the government officials who might have their power stripped away, and even the lowliest workers in tech who rely on the systems to earn their livelihood—all of them will be affected. Each has their own needs and fears, and he imagines having conversations with them about his decision. What arguments would they make? How would they respond if they knew the immense burden resting upon him?

Focusing on the individual consequences of each option also gives rise to potential solutions. If he were to inform the public about the impending chaos that comes with activating the kill switch, perhaps they would be better prepared. He could rally citizens to take action, organizing community networks to help one another during the transition. This could mitigate some of the overwhelming effects that might follow. Printing flyers, organizing meetings, and using underground channels to spread the word might help create a structured support system.

Alex finds himself grappling with the ethical ramifications of his choice. Activating the kill switch might seem like a noble act, but its collateral damage must be considered. In contrast, leaving The Order's control intact contributes to the continuation of their oppressive regime. The ethical debate intensifies, forcing Alex to weigh the lesser of two evils. He realizes that no matter what he chooses, innocent people will suffer. This realization only adds to the weight he carries.

Finally, amidst the turmoil in his mind, Alex has a moment of clarity. He understands that decisions often come with a mix of good and bad outcomes. The key lies in finding a path that prioritizes the greater good while acknowledging the inevitable struggles that accompany change. Perhaps this moment is an opportunity for growth—not just for him but for everyone who has felt the weight of oppression.

In the end, the urgency of the situation pushes him closer to a decision. The longer he hesitates, the greater the risk of losing everything he has fought for. With a deep breath, he steps forward, ready to make his choice. The weight of the world seems to rest upon his shoulders, and yet, in this moment, Alex knows he is prepared for something monumental. Whether he activates the kill switch or chooses to maintain the status quo, the decision will ignite a new chapter in the ongoing fight against The Order.

Chapter 28: The Collapse

The moment the kill switch is activated, the entire system begins its descent into chaos. Everything that relied on technology flickers and falls silent. In a matter of seconds, lights go dark in cities, and screens go blank in homes and offices. The world, once buzzing with the energy of constant communication and connectivity, plunges into a chaotic blackout. This is the moment everyone feared but hoped would never happen. It feels like a nightmare, but it is all too real. Nations, businesses, and communities find themselves suddenly vulnerable, scrambling to navigate a world stripped of its digital backbone.

As the power struggles to stay active for just a bit longer, people begin to panic. Traffic lights fail. Streets become a jumble of cars stopped in their tracks, with drivers honking and shouting, trying to make sense of the unexpected halt. Emergency services struggle to respond, as their communication systems also fall silent. It is a world where the expected order has crumbled and chaos reigns. The consequences of this blackout extend beyond mere inconvenience; they reach into every facet of daily life.

In homes across the globe, families face a stark reality. Children, who often rely on tablets for entertainment, are left with nothing to do. Meals that depend on smart appliances become a chore as cooking methods revert to the old ways. People gather around candles and flashlights, sharing stories and playing games that don't rely on technology. In a strange turn of events, this blackout brings families closer. They discover the value of face-to-face interaction, sharing laughter and concerns without the noise of notifications interrupting their moments.

Meanwhile, the economy takes a significant hit. Businesses that depend on online sales and digital transactions are left helpless. Small shops that have embraced e-commerce suddenly find themselves struggling. The bustling sound of cash registers is replaced with silence. Employers grapple with the decision to send their employees home or try to keep things running without their digital support systems. Stress looms thick in the air as financial losses mount, and uncertainty blankets the future.

Nations begin to scramble in efforts to regain control. Governments mobilize teams to investigate the extent of the collapse, seeking to understand the how and why. Leaders convene emergency meetings, trying to devise a plan amidst the confusion. Citizens are urged to remain calm, but it is easier said than done. Fear creeps into communities. Without the digital infrastructure that society has come to rely on, essential services like water and electricity become dispersed. People must understand how to conserve resources and maintain essential functions without the benefits of automatic systems.

In rural areas, some are better prepared. Those with a background in farming or self-sufficiency begin to lead their communities. People gather to learn about food preservation techniques, and the art of foraging becomes more relevant than ever. Workshops form in town squares, teaching skills that have long been forgotten in the face of technology. Neighbors share tools and resources, showcasing the importance of community and collaboration in times of crisis.

Communication, or the lack thereof, becomes a critical issue. Social media, which is often a lifeline, has gone silent. As rumors spread about the cause of the blackout, communities turn to old-fashioned methods of communication. Bulletin boards in town squares become essential stations for sharing updates. People write down information and pass it out to others, creating a web of knowledge that spreads slowly but effectively. Trusted neighbors become the new sources of information, crafting a sense of unity amid chaos.

Power outages lead to security concerns. With no surveillance to monitor activities, crime rates rise as desperation kicks in. People find themselves grappling with the need to protect their homes and belongings. Town watches become a norm as communities take steps to safeguard themselves. Groups begin to form, patrolling streets at night, lending a sense of security in an increasingly unpredictable world. Bridges are formed as neighbors count on each other for protection and guidance.

Education suffers as well. Schools close their doors, unable to function without their digital tools for lessons and communication. Teachers strive to adapt, crafting plans for non-digital learning. They organize meetups in parks where students can gather for outdoor lessons. This shift reminds everyone of the joy of learning in a natural environment, highlighting nature's beauty as a backdrop for education. Creativity flourishes as students bond over group projects, pouring their thoughts onto paper instead of screens.

As the chaos continues, experts in different fields scramble to devise a solution. Engineers come together to brainstorm ways to restore basic functions without relying on the digital infrastructure. Technicians dive into repairing essential systems while learning from the failure of technology that society had once taken for granted. Their collaboration becomes crucial in devising alternatives to restore order. In labs and garages, inventors work on creating new, simpler technologies that do not depend on the same fragile systems that just crumbled.

Deliveries of essential goods come to a halt as supply chains break down. Hypermarkets face shortages, and the shelves quickly empty as shoppers rush to stock up on necessities. People learn to adapt by connecting with local farmers for fresh produce. Community gardens emerge, bringing people together as they cultivate crops manually, teaching the value of hard work and patience.

With every passing day, different strengths within communities begin to emerge. People remember the skills and trades of old while learning new ones, forging a new path forward. The sense of connection and dependence on technology loses its grip, and a new way of life begins to take shape. Individuals recognize the value of simple skills—cooking, sewing, hunting, and sharing knowledge become tools for survival.

As they nurture their new way of living, discussions arise about future society. People reflect on what went wrong and begin to envision how to rebuild. The digital age, often seen as a beacon of progress, shifts into a topic of debate. Many propose a balance between technology and traditional ways of living. The collapse forces them to reconsider priorities and possibly work towards a future that embraces both worlds.

Through this process, a sense of hope develops amidst the ruins of digital dependence. The community thrives on collaboration, prompting individuals to consider how they can contribute toward enhancing their environment. Rebuilding becomes symbolic of change. Real connections blossom as talents blend and merge into plans for a more resilient future.

As the sun rises on yet another day in a collapsed world, people step out to face the future. The echoes of chaos begin to fade, replaced by a sense of purpose. Through communal effort and shared experiences, they tackle the challenges ahead, united by the knowledge gained from their dark journey. The process of readjustment starts with simple habits, but together, they create a foundation for a stronger, more connected community, ready to face whatever comes next.

Chapter 29: Aftermath

In the wake of the digital collapse, Alex and Eve find themselves surrounded by the remnants of a world that once thrived on technology. The chaos has left behind not only shattered devices but also a sense of loss and uncertainty. They sit together in the dim light of a once-busy café, now eerily quiet, each lost in their thoughts. The whir of machines and the constant buzz of notifications, which used to fill their lives, have vanished. It is a strange feeling, being disconnected from the digital realm that had dominated their daily existence. They turn to each other, both seeking comfort and trying to make sense of what has just happened.

The events that led to this moment swirl in their minds. They remember how the Order, a powerful group that thrived on controlling information and technology, was at the heart of their struggles. With the digital systems in ruins, the Order is no longer the same. Their structures are in disarray, and many of their followers have scattered, lost in the confusion. However, Alex and Eve know that remnants of the Order still exist, lurking in the shadows. This realization brings a mix of fear and determination. They understand that they must remain vigilant, as the fight for freedom is far from over.

As night falls, the café transforms into a refuge, a place where Alex and Eve can share their thoughts and concerns. They discuss the fight they just faced, reflecting on their decisions and the paths they chose. Each decision seemed small at first in a world dominated by technology, but now it weighs heavily on them. They realize that their struggle was not just against the Order, but against a way of living that had become so dependent on technology. They begin to feel a strange kind of empowerment in this realization. The world may be uncertain, but it also offers a chance for change.

They ponder what the future might hold without the comfort of machines. This prompts a conversation about how they can adapt to this new reality. They think about the skills they once overlooked, those that do not rely on the digital world. For instance, Alex recalls how his grandfather taught him to fix machines with his hands, a skill he never thought he would need. Eve shares her passion for gardening, explaining how nurturing plants has taught her patience and the value of life in simple forms. These discussions spark something in them—a desire to reconnect with the world around them.

With the dawn of a new day, Alex and Eve set out to explore their surroundings. They notice the changes in their environment, from the absence of screens to the vibrant sounds of nature. It feels refreshing to breathe in the air untainted by technology. They decide to visit the local library, a place that once seemed old-fashioned but now feels like a treasure trove of knowledge. Their exploration leads them to dusty shelves filled with books that contain stories and information that span many years. These books represent a world that thrived without the constant interference of screens, a world of imagination and creativity.

In the library, they find themselves lost in tales of courage and adventure. As they read, they discuss what they learn and how these lessons might apply to their current situation. They bond over the characters' resilience, drawing parallels to their fight against the Order. Alex points out how many heroes faced seemingly insurmountable odds but found a way to triumph through teamwork and trust. This notion of camaraderie resonates deeply with them; they know that moving forward will require solidarity and support from one another and from the community they hope to rebuild.

To restore hope, they decide to engage with others who share their experiences. They begin seeking out like-minded individuals, forming a small group dedicated to rebuilding their society. This community starts with their friends and neighbors, all of whom have undergone their own struggles. Together, they share ideas and resources, brainstorming ways to adapt to the new reality. They explore the concept of creating a communal space, where everyone can contribute their skills and knowledge, fostering an environment of collaboration. This initiative brings excitement, a spark of positivity in a world that feels bleak.

In their meetings, Alex notices how vital communication is, especially now when misunderstandings can lead to division. They establish a set of guidelines for open discussions, ensuring everyone's voice is heard. This process helps to build trust among group members, laying a foundation for healthy relationships. They find that sharing personal stories not only strengthens their bond but also encourages others to participate. As the community grows, they become more resourceful, pooling their knowledge and skills. They decide to host workshops where people can learn practical skills, such as cooking, repairing items, or even crafting.

Eve takes the lead in organizing gardening workshops, recalling her own childhood experiences. She believes that working with the earth can be therapeutic and rewarding. The first workshop sees a diverse mix of participants gathering in a vacant lot, eager to learn and share. Together, they plant seeds and build raised beds, fostering a sense of community and purpose. As they work together, laughter and conversation fill the air. Even without their screens, they discover joy in connecting with one another and nurturing something tangible.

Meanwhile, Alex reflects on the impact of their actions and the importance of teaching others about the dangers of dependency on technology. He begins to research the history of technology and its evolution, noting both the benefits and drawbacks. He shares his findings with the group, emphasizing the value of balance. He cautions against slipping back into old habits of over-reliance. His insights resonate with the community, igniting discussions about responsible usage of technology, especially when they eventually reintroduce it into their lives.

As weeks pass, Alex and Eve witness the transformation of their community. What started as a small group has blossomed into a vibrant network of individuals connecting on different levels. People share their skills, helping one another in learning and growth. They begin to understand that this new society is not merely about survival but also about living fulfilled lives. Relationships deepen, and friendships emerge. The laughter that once echoed from screens is now present in the conversations they share.

Throughout this journey, the remnants of the Order linger in Alex and Eve's minds. They know that not everyone will embrace the changes they advocate for. There will always be those who resist, holding onto the power the old systems afforded them. This acknowledgment stirs a sense of resolve within Alex and Eve. They recognize that their community will need to be prepared to stand firm against any remnants of the Order. This fuels their motivation to continue building a strong foundation, one defined by solidarity, empathy, and clear communication.

Chapter 30: A New Threat

As the dust settles around Alex, a sense of relief washes over him. The chaos that had engulfed his life is momentarily subdued. He thinks about what he has just experienced, reflecting on the trials he has faced. But just as he begins to feel a sense of normalcy, his phone buzzes on the table next to him. He glances down and sees a new encrypted message. It's from an unknown source, which makes his heart race. The last time he received such a message, it brought a whirlwind of destruction and betrayal. The tension is back, and he knows he must tread carefully.

Alex hesitates before opening the message. He understands that he cannot afford to ignore it. His instincts tell him that there might be more danger lurking in the shadows. Slowly, he types in the decryption key—a series of numbers and letters he has memorized over time. As the message reveals itself, Alex's eyes widen in disbelief. The writing is stark and urgent. It conveys a sense of dread that tightens in his stomach. The Order, the menacing organization he thought was his greatest threat, is not alone. There are other players in the game, and their ambitions loom larger.

The message goes on to outline a conspiracy that reaches global proportions. Alex reads about groups whose interests intersect in dark ways, striving for control over not just power, but information itself. It seems that The Order was merely a small piece in a much larger puzzle. Alex recalls the information he previously gathered. The connections he had suspected are now clearer. He realizes that this goes far beyond his personal struggles. This is a war for control that ultimately seeks to influence the future of humanity.

Yet who are these new players? The message does not provide names, only vague references to covert meetings and alliances. It hints at organizations with significant resources and influence. This makes Alex feel even more isolated. The burden of knowledge weighs heavily on him. Understanding that he must get to the bottom of this situation, he begins brainstorming where to start. He decides to reach out to past allies who might have insights into this broader conspiracy.

First, he thinks of Ava, the brilliant hacker who had been instrumental in his previous encounters. She had always had a knack for digging deep into networks and uncovering hidden secrets. The last time they spoke was on shaky terms, but desperate times call for desperate measures. Alex types a message to her, hoping she will receive it well. In the message, he elaborates on what he discovered and expresses his need for her expertise.

Next, Alex considers reaching out to David, a journalist with connections that often lead to information that others cannot access. David has a nose for news and has uncovered stories about various groups trying to manipulate situations behind the scenes. His voice swirled in Alex's head as he thought about all those discussions they had shared over countless cups of coffee. Alex types another message, hoping that David will take him seriously. After sending both messages, he paces anxiously in his small apartment, waiting for responses.

While he waits, Alex takes a moment to reflect on everything that has happened. The Order had changed his life drastically. He had learned how to fight and adapt, and now he was faced with a new challenge. He needed to learn more about this conspiracy that stretched across the globe and involved various factions. But where does one even begin to find the truth in such a complex web of deceit? The enormity of his task looms over him, but he decides that he cannot allow fear to dictate his actions.

In his search for information, he recalls a smaller group he had encountered during his earlier escapades. They had shown a willingness to share information with him, and perhaps they would have leads on this larger threat. Alex opens his laptop again, going through notes from past encounters. As he tools through pages of half-finished thoughts and leads, a name stands out—The Silent Consensus. This group is rumored to consist of former members of various organizations, all disillusioned by the actions of those in power. They had taken a quiet, yet assertive stance on influencing change, which could now tie into this new threat.

Alex decides he needs to connect with them. He recalls their past gatherings, secretive meetings held in dimly lit venues. It is not easy to gain entry into these underground circles, and he needs to tread carefully. But if they have insights into the larger conspiracy, it could be invaluable. He sets to work crafting a plan, detailing how to gain their trust quickly. Perhaps this time he might even be able to turn allies from his previous foes.

As the minutes tick by, he finally receives a response. Ava is on board. She indicates that she has also sensed a shift in the digital landscape. There are whispers about increased activity within various networks. They agree to meet in person to discuss what she has uncovered. The anticipation builds inside Alex. He feels the urgency and knows they must act quickly before the conspiracy unfolds further.

Shortly after, David replies, somewhat skeptical but intrigued. He wants to meet and discuss the strange happenings he has been covering. This is a positive sign. Both leads align with his growing understanding of the situation. With each message exchanged, Alex feels a jolt of hope. Maybe this fight isn't one he has to face alone. He can feel the pieces starting to align, even as they are scattered across the board.

Determined to confront this new threat, Alex begins organizing his next steps. He knows he must gather information swiftly to piece together the hidden truths. He takes careful notes and makes calls to contacts he hasn't spoken with in a while. He remembers that every detail counts, no matter how trivial it may seem. Every scrap of information can lead to revelations that might prevent a much larger disaster.

He formats his notes into a coherent plan, outlining who he will contact, what he will ask, and how he can ensure the safety of those involved. A sense of focus replaces his earlier anxiety. The urgency of the situation fans the flames of his determination. The world he is facing is larger than he had anticipated, filled with dangerous players and chilling intentions. But Alex realizes that knowledge is his most powerful weapon.

In the days that follow, he immerses himself in this investigation, leveraging his connections and using resources he didn't even realize he had at his disposal. Each encounter pulls him deeper into this dark web of conspiracies. The tension builds, as does the realization that he is engaged in a fight that may reshape the future. Alex understands that this new threat is just the beginning of something much larger.

www.ingramcontent.com/pod-product-compliance
Lightning Source LLC
Chambersburg PA
CBHW050306230526
45471CB00005B/2040